The Living Community

A Venture into Ecology

Also by S. Carl Hirsch

THE GLOBE FOR THE SPACE AGE
THIS IS AUTOMATION
FOURSCORE... AND MORE: THE LIFE SPAN OF MAN
PRINTING FROM A STONE: THE STORY OF LITHOGRAPHY

Illustrated by William Steinel

Hirsch, S Carl

S. Carl Hirsch

The Living Community

A Venture into Ecology

The Viking Press / New York

For a very special person,
Eleanor Leander

[1967, c 1966]

First published in 1966 by The Viking Press, Inc.
625 Madison Avenue, New York, N. Y. 10022
Published simultaneously in Canada by
The Macmillan Company of Canada Limited
Library of Congress catalog card number: 66-14415
574.5 Ecology
Second printing April 1967

PRINTED IN THE U.S.A. BY HALLIDAY LITHOGRAPH CORP.

Acknowledgments

To a number of outstanding scientists in the field of ecology, I would like to express my appreciation for their painstaking efforts to improve the manuscript. These include: Dr. Marston Bates, Department of Zoology, University of Michigan; Dr. W. Frank Blair, Department of Zoology, University of Texas; Dr. LaMont C. Cole, Chairman, Department of Zoology, Cornell University; Dr. Paul B. Sears, Department of Biology, Yale University.

Others to whom I am indebted for their suggestions and encouragement are: Dr. Clarence and Marie Goodnight of the Department of Biological Sciences, Western Michigan University; James M. Lockart, Education Representative, Illinois Department of Conservation; Clifford E. Emanuelson, Pinchot Institute for Studies in Conservation. I am also grateful to the following: Dr. Charles E. Olmsted, Chairman, and Harold Gall, of the Department of Botany, University of Chicago; Dr. Eugene P. Odum, Department of Zoology, University of Georgia; Dr. John F. Reed, President, Fort Lewis College; Dr. Robert B. Platt, Department of Biology, Emory University; Dr. Stephen H. Spurr, Dean of the School of Graduate Studies, University of Michigan; John H. Wolfe, Chief of the Environmental Services Branch of the Division of Biology and Medicine, U. S. Atomic Energy Commission.

In addition, I appreciate the help from naturalists and the staffs of U. S. Government bureaus, of state departments of conservation, of zoological and botanical institutions, who supplied factual information concerning ecological problems.

Contents

The Living Community

A Venture into Ecology

1. Town in the Forest

Nature will bear the closest inspection. She invites us to lay our eye level with her smallest leaf, and take an insect view of its plain.
—HENRY DAVID THOREAU

Every town has its secrets. And a passing stranger may wonder: Who lives here? How do the residents make their living? Why did they choose this place?

The town may be one of the man-made towns, strung out like knots that tie together a fishnet of country roads.

Or the town may be deep in the forest. Its exact location may be a bog, or a cave, or a hillock, or a hollow log.

A dead log may, in fact, be rich with life. Here a thousand varied creatures live, making up a community. In some brisk autumn dawn, these log-dwellers stir. Ebony crickets and green-gold beetles forage busily for food. The last wildflowers of the year strain toward the dwindling sun. A crab spider scurries out of the range of a passing lizard, back to its web.

Within a hive in the log cavity, an aging queen of bees is already in winter sleep, full of the eggs she will lay in the spring. A caterpillar wraps itself carefully into a cocoon. And the log rot gives slow growth to living molds and mosses.

In a burrow formed when the falling oak tore itself from the earth, a chipmunk family breakfasts on a windfall of seeds and berries.

This is the Logtown community. Here a toad shares citizenship with a toadstool. The redbud is neighbor to a green snake curled against the warmth of the decaying log. Countless other creatures live here that are visible only through a magnifying lens.

From the eye level of an insect, this community bustles with activity. Like the human community, it has its share of quarrels, its small tragedies, its daily rhythm of food-gathering, resting, mating, homemaking, family-raising.

The tenants of the log are not as separate as they may seem. They are each and all members of a real community, bound to one another in countless ways. Their town has a definite form and pattern.

The forest is filled with such towns, all parts of the wider woodland community. And just as there are towns in the forest, so there are cities in the sea and villages on the prairie. Of all the communities on this planet, only the smallest number is peopled by human beings.

A wide range of animals may share lightless lives in the permanent darkness of a deep cave—all of them whitish and blind. Strange bedfellows may be found living in the cavities of a sea sponge. An interesting group of creatures may make their home together on some rocky crag. The communities in the rain forest harbor a rich variety of living things. And still

another type of community is the tiny sea island where assorted beings live in the shadow of a smoldering volcano.

Wherever such wildlife communities appear, they stir the same haunting questions: Who and how and why? These towns in nature are webbed with a thousand mysteries.

But the probing questions are not idle ones for human beings to ask. Our own lives are woven deeply into the answers.

Nature withheld few secrets from the American poet-naturalist Henry David Thoreau. He was a Harvard graduate, class of 1837. Some of his classmates went into law, others into the ministry. Thoreau took to the woods.

"Many a forenoon have I stolen away," he recounted, "preferring to spend thus the most valued part of the day; for I was rich, if not in money, in sunny hours and summer days, and spent them lavishly."

He described himself as self-appointed inspector of rainstorms, surveyor of forest paths, and keeper of the wildstock.

He roamed Indian-style through the woods. His pockets bulged with the gear of the naturalist—a spyglass, a jackknife, twine, and a small microscope. He carried an old music book for pressing plants, and a notebook in which he captured the sights and sounds of the wildlife in soaring poetry or in singing prose.

Thoreau built a tiny cabin on Walden Pond near Concord, Massachusetts. There he enjoyed the company of woodsmen and woodchucks. And there he practiced his chosen profession —observing nature in a special way.

"You only need sit still long enough in some attractive spot in the woods that all its inhabitants may exhibit themselves to you by turns," he wrote.

It was in this fashion that Thoreau became a part of the natural community.

He was not a specialist in any species, nor was he a great collector or experimenter. He had no laboratory other than the "sweet wild world" of the woodland itself.

He was an eyewitness of the order and the activity in the natural community. He could look at a neighbor's field, enjoy its interplay, and then remark as he did once, "I had no idea that there was so much going on in Haywood's meadow."

Many of nature's secrets are discovered only in this kind of broad view. Some of the most puzzling events of the woodland are explained only as plants and animals are observed living together against the natural setting of the soil and the season. Certain facts about species can be learned only within the context of the free-flowing life of the natural community.

On a spring night in the year 1842, Thoreau found himself on a strange woodland adventure. As he poled his boat gently across a silent New England pond, his pine torch lit up the scene below. To his delight, the crystal depths appeared like a living city, its roofs raised to reveal the private community of the fishes.

"There they lie in every variety of posture," he later wrote, "some on their backs with their white bellies uppermost, some suspended in mid-water, some sculling gently along with a dreamy motion of the fins, and others quite active and wide awake—a scene not unlike what the human city could present. . . ."

Thoreau's genius was in seeing life whole. One can learn much about a clock by taking it apart—but not find its tick. Thoreau observed nature in its wholeness instead of piecemeal, learned its rhyme and its rhythm.

There is an old nursery rhyme that begins with the loss of a horseshoe nail. Inevitably, this small cause leads to the loss of a battle, and finally to the loss of a kingdom.

In similar fashion, every small happening in nature touches off other happenings. Spring thaw and rock slide, the birth of a fawn, the fall of an oak—such events set up a series of results within the living community. From a single cause flows a running stream of effects.

A poet once said that one could not pluck a flower without troubling a star. This is another way of saying that the living and the nonliving are all linked together. Lives are altered by changing temperature, climate, and moisture, by the very shape of the land and the chemicals that are in it.

The courses of streams are shifted by dam-building beavers. Rock is turned into soil by the action of frost and plants, of water and small animals. The population of mosquitoes is reduced by the first cold snap. An entire forest may be set ablaze by a flash of lightning.

The naturalist Charles Darwin had a story to illustrate the

endless chain of causes and effects. In Great Britain, he pointed out, roaming cats eat field mice at the edge of town. It seems that the quantity of wild bumblebees is controlled by the mice, which destroy their nests. If the mouse population is kept down by the cats, then there are more bees to pollinate the red clover plants. As a result of all this, the British fields are deep in clover.

Others playfully added to Darwin's story. British beef cattle grow fat on clover. And the British navy thrives on beef. Old maids become more plentiful as the navy takes more men for sea duty. And old maids like to keep cats. Put it all together and it would seem that old maids are responsible for Britain's naval might!

In dealing with nature, man is often puzzled by strange turns of events. Simple but unseen causes may lead to hunger and disease, to crop failure and human tragedy.

The people of Ireland were once dependent on the potato as their main source of food. The summer of 1845 proved to be a poor one for potato-growing. It was a good year for a tiny fungus that destroys potatoes.

In the tragic days that followed, famine struck the island nation. When it was all over, a million people had died. Two million more had been forced to leave their homeland.

A chain of events may be touched off by man's own doings. It may begin with the crack of a rifle or the bite of an ax.

An upland forest is cleared of trees. The area is turned into a pasture which soon becomes over-grazed and bare. Now the rain water is no longer held in the ground by the deep roots of trees and shrubs. Instead, the water runs swiftly off the surface, forming gullies. On the hillside farms the good wells run dry. In the valleys below, the spring torrents rush wildly together, flooding the countryside.

The explanation of such events that have long baffled mankind seems tangled in a thousand threads. Today scientific study is beginning to unravel some of the old problems and many new ones as well. The science of causes and effects in the natural community is called ecology.

One of the newer branches of biology, ecology is concerned with the associations of living and nonliving things. It begins its study of life—as Thoreau did—in the wildlife communities, seeking answers to important problems in the patterns of nature.

The work of the ecologist has sometimes been called "the science of everything." He is absorbed with the "why" of nature. Usually, the answer is contained in a thousand bits and fragments of fact. His clues may be as varied as the flyways of geese or the surge of an underground stream, the busy work of bacteria or the damming of a river.

The behavior of living things is often strange and complicated. But certain patterns of life do repeat themselves. An orderly design can be discovered. Developments can be predicted. Events can be understood.

The methods of the ecologist, like those of other scientists, begin with the careful observation of the facts. Precise information is gathered, checked and rechecked endlessly. Out of a large body of data emerges a small but growing set of scientific principles.

The name "ecology" was formed about a hundred years ago out of the Greek word *oikos,* which means "home." Ecology is the study of the home life of living things, how they relate to one another and to their nonliving environment.

The ecologist works in the laboratory. But he can probably be found most often in the field. He may be taking a census of earthworms. Or he may be investigating the ecology of high altitudes, the towers of the earth where communities of living things survive the low atmospheric pressure, the intense cold, and the relative scarcity of oxygen.

He may study how the population of the arctic fox varies with the population of lemmings or how the number of red oaks in a forest depends on the number of acorn-burying squirrels.

In its quiet beginnings, the new science of ecology is becoming an important problem-solver. It is more than that. It is the growing edge of our understanding about the living fabric of nature.

The life of the seas and the uplands, of the prairies and the forests, is a web of species. In some places the fabric is time-tested and strong. In other places the weave is loose and can be unraveled by the tearing of a single thread. At times, the texture within a particular region is richly patterned. Or else it may be riddled and threadbare.

Woven throughout the fabric of life is man, the dominant species. To the ecologist, man is increasingly important in the whole design of living things. Ecology deals realistically with the web of life as it has been changed by human beings.

The ecologist may investigate the number of acres of prairie that will properly support a herd of sheep. His main interest may be the health of an olive grove or an oyster bed. His searches may take him to the gloomy sea depths, where natural communities tend to be stable and a few of them may have existed since the beginnings of life on earth. Or he may be at work on the problems of an entirely new kind of community—the life-support system aboard a spaceship.

A group of ecologists at a Midwestern university have set up a tiny living community. This tightly sealed "hothouse" is the experimental mock-up for some future spacecraft. This is the kind of community that may be used to sustain life on an expedition to the moon or a visit to a neighboring planet.

Small mammals and insects, assorted grasses and shrubs live inside, amid apparatus and instruments. The animal life is being carefully studied to determine its needs. The plants are chosen to purify the air, to reclaim waste materials, and to offer high yields of suitable foods in a limited growing area.

This is a "closed system," where plants and animals are in metabolic balance. Each form of life sustains the other, and each makes use of what the other produces.

The essentials for long-time support of life are the same everywhere—whether in an outpost flung into space or in some wild place in the forest. These communities are microcosms, small worlds where plants and animals share life together.

2. Beings Need Beings

I am singled out and separated as it were, from all the world, to be miserable. . . . I am divided from mankind. . . . I have no soul to speak to.
—DANIEL DEFOE, *Robinson Crusoe*

Nothing lives alone. The hermit crab shares its borrowed snail-shell home with other creatures. Despite its name the so-called solitary sandpiper is a bird that is seldom seen alone. And the "lone" wolf is usually a member of a pack. Even the human hermit in a mountain shack is tied to his fellow men by thousands of unseen threads.

There are group names for wildlife—herds and packs, swarms and schools, coveys and flocks. Many birds nest together. Bats sleep together. Herring feed together. Butterflies migrate together.

Beings seem drawn to one another. The hunter has learned

that, simply by making the sound of a duck, he attracts other ducks.

Against an autumn sky, gray geese appear like a single arrow in flight. Great numbers of gulls, mackerel, wild buffalo, move with such unity and precision that each individual seems to merge into the larger body.

Honeybees keep an orderly home life. In bee societies, the members are grouped according to their duties. The colony includes bees specialized in producing the offspring, foraging for food, maintaining and guarding the hive, as well as those in immature stages. From birth, bees follow the highly organized work pattern of the hive.

There are similar societies of ants, termites, and wasps. Such social groups of insects outlast the lives of individual members and continue on for generations. These are societies of blood relatives, all of them descended from one "queen" or from a "royal couple."

However, there are also organized groups of animals that are much broader than a single family. Shoals of herring, droves of caribou, coveys of partridges are each a society of many families of the same species.

It is not only birds of a feather that flock together. Differing species live in close unity as well.

A great many types of partnership exist in nature—plant with plant, animal with animal, and plant with animal. Some of these relationships are strange and unusual. Others are as familiar as the arrangement by which a honeybee helps a flower to produce seeds, and gets the ingredients for its honey in return.

For both the bee and the plant, this is a matter of life and death. Neither could survive without the other.

In many daily acts of life, there are advantages for the

member of the group. Wolves are able to hunt more successfully when they do so in packs. Bees benefit when a scout returns from foraging and by certain sounds and movements alerts the entire hive to a new source of food. Beavers are able to construct a system of dams through the cooperation of an entire colony.

Dependent behavior and mutual aid form the basis of well-ordered communities made up of many families, many societies, many partnerships, as well as countless transients that may become part of the community for only a brief stay or a particular season. The community also is dependent on important nonliving features—soil and moisture, the air and light, and the special conditions of altitude, climate, and living space.

Plants and animals need many things from their environment. These demands differ widely. Some beings require a wet living area, and others are suited to the desert. Some plants cannot exist without bright sunlight, while others live in darkness. Some animals must have lots of room for roaming, and others thrive in crowded conditions.

Organisms also need each other. Few living things can survive for long without the living group and the living community.

Social life offers advantages in fulfilling two important needs —food and safety.

In *Alice in Wonderland,* Lewis Carroll describes the crocodile:

> How cheerfully he seems to grin,
> How neatly spreads his claws,
> And welcomes little fishes in
> With gently smiling jaws!

Such an attitude in the natural community may seem unneighborly. How can you have your community—and eat it?

Strangely enough, the eating habits of the crocodile are part of a way of life that has kept order on this planet for several million years.

By their appetites, species keep some kind of control on other species. If rats or rabbits, larks or locusts, multiplied without any check, they would soon become too numerous for their own good.

The codfish lays millions of eggs. But if codfish eggs and small cod were not eaten by other sea dwellers, the ocean would be a solid mass of cod.

Foxes that depend on rabbits for food keep the number of rabbits in check. And the limited population of rabbits in turn imposes a limit on the number of foxes.

It is easy to mistake the meaning of mealtime in the wilds. It often seems that living species are bent on destroying one another. But a species that exterminated other species on which it depended for food would itself cease to exist. Species and communities do survive through the natural patterns by which plants, insects, and animals are harvested. Plants that are ripe and animals that are old are usually the first to be taken for food. A hawk can easily pick off a laggard bird or mouse. And wolves usually feed on the straggling members of the deer herd.

Animals seek food that fits the needs of their bodies, that is easily available, that suits their tastes, that is of the proper size. Some favor certain types of plants. Others prey on other animals.

The hawk, with its body requirements for meat, has little choice. Either it hunts or dies.

Such predatory animals live on smaller animals. Some small

organisms live as parasites on bigger ones. At times, the predator may become the prey of an even larger animal. An insect parasite may itself become the host for parasites of microscopic size.

There are forms of animal life that are parasites on plants. And there are plants that live as parasites on animals. Man is himself a natural predator, living on the meat of mammals, fish, and fowl, as well as on plants.

All living things are in a constant search for nourishment. As the spider weaves a net to snare its prey, so the cherry tree spreads its leaves to catch the sunlight and its roots tap the underground water and draw in minerals from the soil.

The sun is the source of energy for life. But only green plants have the ability to use the energy of sunlight to manufacture energy-filled foods from inorganic matter—carbon dioxide and water. Green plants alone can produce the organic materials out of which both plant and animal tissues are constructed. Hence, the animal kingdom must live on other living things, with both plants and animals serving as food. Solar energy, passing from one organism to another in the form of food, links all life together.

Only if a blade of grass is eaten by a cricket, which in turn is eaten by a frog, which is eaten by a snake, and the snake becomes the prey of an eagle on high—only then will the soaring eagle find the supply of sun-born energy stored in the blade of grass.

The food chain begins with the green plant. Next in line comes a plant eater. One, two, or three meat eaters may follow in the chain of nourishment that ties the natural community together.

Chemical substances that support life circulate in great cyclic paths through the plant and animal community. Such matter is transferred from one organism to another in soil, air, and water. Moving through these media, and repeatedly relayed through living organisms, these molecules are used and re-used, broken down and reconstructed.

In this process, an important function is played by those forms of life which feed on dead things. Soil bacteria, fungi, and molds decompose dead organisms and waste matter and release chemical substances that may be used again in the cycles of life.

Nitrogen compounds in plants, used as foods, form the important animal proteins. Given off by animals in waste materials, nitrogen enters the soil, is stored up again in plant tissues, and then is relayed back to animals. In dramatic fashion, the nitrogen cycle reveals how dependent the various parts of the living community are on one another. Although nitrogen is present in the air for animals to breathe, most animal life is unable to fulfill its nitrogen needs in that way. Most plants cannot utilize the nitrogen in the air or in dead organic matter in the soil until it is converted into certain compounds. These compounds are formed by the activities of several types of microorganisms, which make this essential nutrient available to plants for their growth. Nitrogen thus enters into the food chains, and animals can secure the nitrogen they need in order to survive.

Along with nitrogen, many other essential chemical elements are circulated through plants and animals by means of similar cycles.

With each breath of life, animals absorb oxygen from the air and give off carbon dioxide. In daylight, green plants take in carbon dioxide and in turn release free oxygen into the atmosphere—oxygen which is required by animals, as well as by plants, to liberate energy from food.

The living community is a complex pattern of such give-and-take. In the very processes of fulfilling their own needs for substances in food, water, and air, organisms supply necessary living materials for others. These are the arrangements that bind plant and animal life together.

In Aesop's fable, the fox was being ridiculed by the forest animals for losing the race with a hare he was chasing.

"I was only running for my supper," the fox replied, "while the hare was running for his life."

While some creatures eat others, each individual strives to avoid being eaten. In this effort for survival, many organisms depend strongly on the support of the group, the society, the community.

A covey of bobwhite quails may roost in a tight circle at night. This is their defense not only against attackers but also against storms and severe cold. Similar practices are common among small animals and even insects.

A floating jellyfish with a poisonous sting, the Portuguese man-of-war, is really a colony of marine animals, grouped together for protection and mutual aid.

The musk ox is typical of those large mammals of the plains which stand shoulder-to-shoulder against attacking beasts.

Banded together, members of a single species can often make a strong defense against predators. By a system of scouts and sentinels, entire communities may be warned when to take cover. Along the shoreline, many different creatures are roused to approaching danger by the shrill alarm of the gull.

No species can survive unless it has safe conditions for one important kind of group activity—the raising of a family. Organisms are brought into the world only by other organisms of the same species. In most forms of animal life, the very process of reproduction involves two parents and a varying number of offspring. In many species, the bearing and raising of the young is carried on with the protection of the larger group.

Some animals will reproduce only in the wild. They will not have their young in a zoo, no matter how friendly the zoo-keepers appear to be. Strangely, this includes a few species that are not normally shy of people. Certain squirrels and the house sparrow do not readily breed in cages.

On countless ocean islands and rocky cliffs of remote bays, birds and mammals gather in huge numbers each year. This is the swarming of certain species for the mating season. Sea birds fly thousands of miles, and seals swim long distances, to be at the chosen places at the proper times.

Here mates are selected, breeding takes place, the young are born and given their start in life. Often there seems to be little explanation as to why a certain site was chosen for this activity—except for the features of safety and privacy for the group.

It is common in nature that the reproduction of one species relies on the help of members of another. Sometimes the very survival of a species will depend on such assistance.

The great biologist Charles Darwin once made a study of how plant seeds may be transported for long distances, beyond the carrying power of either wind or water currents. He carefully brushed the mud off the feet of a single bird. Embedded in the mud were many seeds, from which Darwin was able to raise eighty-two plants, belonging to five separate species.

An autumn walk through the prairie will usually reveal the skill of burrs in catching rides on passing animals. Such seed-bearing fruits, with barbed or sticky coverings, are often carried long distances in the fur or feathers of passers-by before they drop off and give rise to new plants where the competition for soil and water is not so intense.

Some flowers are shaped in such a way that an insect cannot get its food without bringing in pollen from another flower and picking up more pollen to be carried to still another one.

Some years ago, a certain fig tree was introduced into California from the Mediterranean region for commercial purposes. It was soon realized, however, that these plants would not reproduce without the fig wasp, which carries the pollen from one fig-tree flower to another.

The bee is the most famous of the insect pollinators. It visits flowers to secure nectar and pollen to be brought back to the hive for food. And certain flowers attract the bees because of their form and color and fragrance. During the course of these visits, tiny pollen grains become attached to the body of the bee. When the bee visits another flower of the same species, some of the pollen is deposited, completing the process of pollination.

Many flowers are completely dependent on the bee in order to reproduce. The monkshood, a bumblebee flower, does not grow wild in North America outside the range of bumblebees.

In some cases, flowers can pollinate themselves. However, there are advantages to the plants when insects transfer the pollen, criss-crossing from the blossom of one plant to that of another. Offspring produced by cross-pollination tend to be hardier, more varied, better able to survive, than those that are the products of self-pollination.

The many ways in which organisms depend on one another find expression in the natural community. The community offers protection to the species, but also presents dangers to the individual organisms. The community provides available food—but also the threat to the unwary creature that it may become food for some predator. The community affords opportunities for raising a family—but never free from the hazards of the wild environment.

Each species finds its own advantages in living together in the natural setting. In the woodland community, the mouse is concealed from the hawk. The thrush fledglings are snug in a tree nest, and fed from a nearby source of food. In the forest, the walking stick can masquerade as a twig. The screech owl finds safety in appearing exactly like the hickory branch on which it perches. Among the shrubs, the fragile columbine is sheltered from the wind.

3. The Turning of the Worm

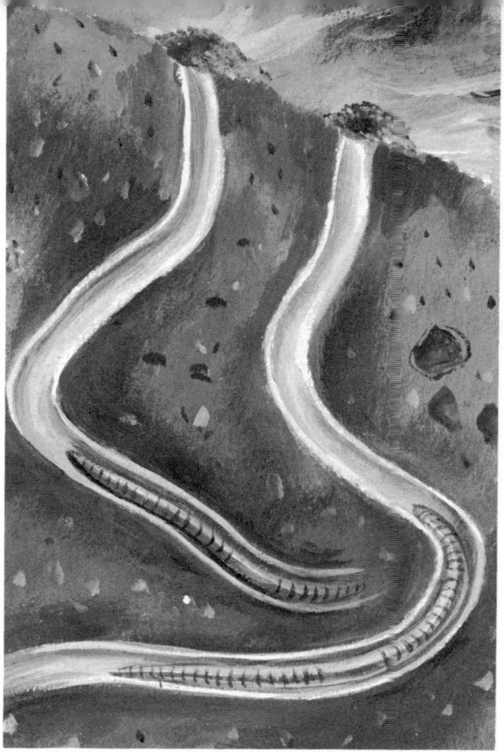

Look abroad thro' Nature's range,
Nature's mighty law is change.
—ROBERT BURNS

"The plough is one of the most ancient and most valuable of man's inventions," Charles Darwin pointed out, "but long before he [man] existed, the land was in fact regularly ploughed, and still continues to be ploughed, by earthworms."

Darwin estimated that, on a single acre of meadow in a single year, earthworms actually bring tons of soil to the surface. These worms make their way down through the soil by swallowing it, and the chemical composition of the soil is changed as it passes through their bodies. Working through the layers, they loosen and transfer the earth. They constantly turn over new leaves, drag them into their burrows, mix them with the old soils.

The earthworm changes the entire community by changing the very soil on which it lives. For all its turning and churning, the worm is only one of the countless changers that transform nature endlessly.

The ecologist skillfully observes the shifting landscape. He looks for causes and effects. He sees nature as dynamic and restless. He finds explanations for present-day patterns of life in slow geologic events of the past such as the shifting of the earth's crust, the changing of regional climates, the movement of glaciers. He tries to "read" the meaning of a migration of animals, of the appearance of a new type of vegetation, or a small change in the weather that may bring an entire set of important results.

In living nature, some changes are repeated regularly. On a stretch of seaside that is bathed twice daily, the beach community lives by the moon rhythm of the tides. A marsh community changes with each rising and setting of the sun. At twilight the throbbing overture of the bullfrog rouses the night-life creatures. As the day shift vanishes, in their place come the salamanders, the night hawks, the fireflies, and the muskrats.

Both plants and animals respond in a variety of ways to the length of the day and night. The duration of sunlight and darkness signals the time for the germination of seeds and the flowering of plants. It also sets off changes in the living habits of animals, determining the time for mating and migration. The fur coat of the ermine turns from brown to white as the autumn days become shorter.

The great wheel of the seasons brings important changes to almost every natural community. The onset of winter finds bats, woodchucks, and frogs sheltered in deep sleep.

When April rouses the woodland again, it is the morning

of the year. In the hush of spring come the wood thrush and the warm rain and the wild crocus. Soon the separated, sealed-in creatures move outward. The sun stirs the seed from its case, the land snail in its shell, the maple bud from its sheath. By reaching movement and by quickening growth, the landscape becomes alive with living beings.

The appearance of much of the woodland is transformed by the patterns of life among broad-leaved trees which shed their leaves in the fall, often with a spectacular display of color. They remain bare through the winter so that no delicate tissues are exposed to frost, and grow new leaves in the spring. This annual sequence in turn affects the plant and animal life that are part of a deciduous-tree community.

Strewn about are fallen leaves the color of dark wine and pale bronze. The soil is being enriched from the decaying foliage and the rotting logs. Here perhaps a new oak will grow. The acorn from which it sprouts may be part of a squirrel's hoard, long buried and forgotten.

New life is here in buds and larvae, seeds and eggs. And there are the husks of old seed pods, the outgrown armor of beetles, the whitened bone of a squirrel, the star-shaped tracks of a bluejay, long since flown.

Nature presents a breathtaking picture of contrasting moods, the colors of insects and birds shifting from somber to brilliant, and plant forms changing from the tight buds of early spring to the full-grown fruits of early autumn.

In the sprawling wilderness of early nineteenth-century America, John James Audubon caught the spirit of the changing forest community in his paintings. From the brush of this artist flowed a matchless portrait of American wildlife.

Unlike naturalist painters before him, Audubon pictured his

subjects as alive and active instead of dead and stuffed. At times, his bedroom in some backwoods hostel was aflutter with birds, live models. Most important of all, he tracked birds and mammals to their natural settings and painted them in their native communities in all the seasons of the year.

Most spectacular of the seasonal changes are the migrations. Some animals move in large groups from their home communities to distant ones.

For centuries, men have marveled over the comings and goings of birds. And in 1803, Audubon wondered about the migrations of the American species. He was eighteen years old and had come to the United States only a short time before. After spending his boyhood in France, he had been sent here to learn business. But his real interest was in the business of falcons and butterflies, buffaloes and phoebes.

Audubon was drawn to a secret place in the forest. The residents of a shallow cave included a brood of phoebes. While sketching them, he pondered the ancient puzzles about these summer birds which were soon to depart.

Before they did, the young artist-naturalist slipped a silver wire band on the leg of each bird. In the months that followed, he waited.

As the spring days lengthened, Audubon returned again and again to the woods near his Pennsylvania home. The community in the little open cave now teemed with wildlife, and soon the bird nests were tenanted again. He observed them carefully and anxiously. Yes, three of the phoebes wore silver bracelets.

In America, no one had ever before banded migrant birds to learn with certainty which of them return year after year to their summer communities.

The tracking of birds has become a highly developed science

and today it is often done by electronic instruments. But the chief means of tracing the migrants is still the banding method used by Audubon. The most common migrating birds of America have been traced across their well-established flyways to the warmer lands where they return repeatedly each year during the winter months.

Of their two homes, their main home community is considered to be the one which is in the coldest part of their range, as it is here that they return to breed and raise their young.

Banding and other identifying methods are used to trace the wanderings of a great variety of creatures—whales and bats, lemmings and locusts, salmon and seals, and monarch butterflies that gather each fall and depart in a colorful cloud.

Animal migration probably is a response to some internal changes in body chemistry, triggered by external changes in the environment. The ecologist tries to find explanations for these large-scale movements in terms of survival patterns. By their travels some creatures avoid cold or drought. Many animals migrate to obtain a better food supply or to breed. While some wintering animals can live on stored food, others must go elsewhere to feed. Some species travel chiefly to a mating and nesting site. Still others do their breeding and feeding at both ends of the migratory route.

The arctic tern is considered to be the most remarkable of migrant birds. It nests on the tundra and on the arctic islands of both hemispheres. Its yearly migration takes this bird as much as ten thousand miles to the Antarctic Circle, later to return northward to its home community. As a result of its movements, the arctic tern experiences more hours of daylight than any other creature known.

For many years, no one knew the winter destination of migrating chimney swifts, which have their nest sites in the chimneys of many American homes. By means of banding, it was learned that these small birds make an annual trip to Peru, South America.

Seals that spend their winters off the coast of California travel three thousand miles to mating grounds in the Pribilof Islands in the North Pacific.

Every two or three years, large numbers of green turtles begin a swimming marathon across the high seas from the coast of Brazil. Their destination is Ascension Island, a barren ocean rock in the Atlantic. To this nesting place, they swim slowly and steadfastly on a true course some fourteen hundred miles eastward.

Some distinction is usually made between fresh-water and salt-water species of fishes. However, the migration of the salmon takes it from the ocean, where it spends its adult life, to spawn in the fresh-water streams. And the eel, which inhabits fresh-water rivers and ponds, is always hatched in the ocean, usually in the large area of the Atlantic called the Sargasso Sea.

How are land animals guided to distant places, often without landmarks, in darkness or under cloudy skies, without leaders that have made the trip before? How do fish, reptiles, and marine mammals navigate the open sea to reach some remote meeting place? How do large swarms of storm-driven insects and birds reach their destinations?

There is as yet no one set of answers that can explain these feats. Scientists are investigating whether the guidance of migrating animals is performed by means of a "sixth" sense or of a special sharpness of one of the familiar senses. They are probing the possibility that some animals have a sense of the earth's magnetic field.

Much evidence points to a built-in "light compass" that permits the travelers to steer by the sun, moon, and stars. But since heavenly bodies appear in different positions at different times of the day and year, there remains the question of whether the migrants also have some sense of time, some biological clock and calendar.

It is possible that different guidance methods are used by various animals and insects, and that each individual uses a combination of means in order to complete its journey.

Among the travelers are those nomads which move from

place to place without necessarily making a round trip. Some are wandering hunters, like coyotes and wolves. Among insects are the locust swarms of the desert areas that seem to move with the winds, devouring every bit of vegetation where they stop to feed.

Some creatures are emigrants, having moved to a new location without ever returning to the old. The cattle egret, a long-time native of Africa and southern Asia, has appeared in the Western Hemisphere during recent years. First seen in Florida in 1948, this egret feeds mainly on ticks, fleas, and grasshoppers that abound in the meadows where cattle graze. Its emigration is considered a success, since it has found its new American home suitable for its favored style of living with cattle.

The travels of large numbers of organisms are usually considered to be a matter of survival. And yet there are well-known cases in which groups of creatures move steadily toward their own destruction. Such is the story of the lemmings of Scandinavia, which periodically set out on a long journey across land's end to drown in the sea.

In the case of the American butterfly called the painted lady, its long spring migration is completed not by those who departed but by later generations born along the way. The 3000-mile flight from its southern range toward Canada is repeatedly halted for egg-laying and the offspring that are born make the next leg of the journey.

The long-distance trips of animals are most spectacular, but countless other transient creatures are on the move as well. Some, such as the army ants, march determinedly cross-country and make only a few yards of progress in a day. Such traffic and movement helps to give endless variety to the natural community.

There is an old saying that one cannot bathe twice in the same stream. All of nature is like the flowing water, continually passing and changing.

The changes are those of growth and decay, birth and death. New settlers appear, others vanish. A food supply gives out. Climates change. A pond dries up. A sand dune shifts.

A stable community may suddenly become a ghost town because its framework has been altered by some havoc.

The volcano Krakatoa exploded on the night of August 27, 1883. Where the Pacific and Indian Oceans meet, the small volcanic island blew up in fire and ash, leaving no trace of its plant or animal life.

The debris that finally settled into the boiling sea formed a new island that became known as the Daughter of Krakatoa.

Nine months later, scientists found a single living thing on this island—a tiny spider spinning a web. Plant seeds and spores carried by the wind or water, and creatures that fly, swim, and float gradually gave back to the island its mantle of life. After eighty years, it is once again a living community, rich with tropical vegetation and animal species.

At times, the long-standing communities of nature are torn apart by fire and flood, by wave and whirlwind. Then the slow process of healing begins.

The shattered community does not immediately reappear as it was. It comes back by a series of stages.

These odd patterns once interested the New England neighbors of Henry David Thoreau and they sought him out. The farmers were puzzled.

Why is it, they wanted to know, that after an oak woodlot is cut down, the first new trees that appear are not oaks, but pines? Thoreau explained it in an essay called "The Succession of Trees."

The naturalist showed how "the wind conveys the seeds of pines into hard woods and open land." These pine seedlings grow on the oak forest floor, but they never get their chance while the oaks dominate the forest.

As long as the oaks remain, their leaves spread to the rainfall and sunlight, forming a broad canopy that keeps the forest floor relatively dark and dry. The network of oak roots absorbs a large volume of the mineral and water sources underground.

If something should happen to the dominant species, lesser plant varieties may get their moment of glory. Tree species that never before went beyond the seedling stage grow to full size. Such a change in the foliage may in turn bring new species of nesting birds. The altering of the available plant foods may impel some insects and small mammals to leave and will attract others.

The science of ecology has made a detailed study of such successions. Ecologists have discovered what happens when a living community is destroyed and different kinds of plants and animals appear, some that seem to be strangers to the area. Such passing stages take place where a pond dries out, where a timberland is burned away, where a shoreline is undercut by the tides. Similar patterns are seen as the first new growths begin to take hold in some barren sand beach, desert area, or dust-filled prairie.

A series of temporary communities grow up and die off. Each makes way for the next. In time, the short-lived settlements disappear and in their place comes something that seems better fitted for that environment.

Stable plant species take firm hold. They root deeply and grow taller. The animals that now appear are hardier. The community comes into its own in a great climax of strong growth and a characteristic mixture of species.

All the residents seem to be made to order for this place. Undisturbed, they form a vigorous community that can live together for a long time, fitting into their surroundings in the most wondrous ways. Even more remarkable is the way in which the species are suited to one another.

In the stable community the chemistry of life is balanced out between plants and animals, and the bacteria that border between them. Here food chains rise from the strong grasses, the busy earthworms, and the small mammals upward to the soaring eagle. Here, the caterpillar that eats a wildflower leaf may in the spring become the butterfly that pollinates that same flower!

The way that species live together can best be observed in the wildlife community. But how did plants and animals begin their social existence? How did community life develop? The answers can be found only as Darwin found them—in the endless process of evolution.

4. Voyage to the Past

"And of every living thing of all flesh, two of every sort shalt thou bring into the ark. . . . Thus did Noah."

—GENESIS

The Darwin story begins (as so many great stories begin) with a young man and a sailing ship.

The H.M.S. *Beagle,* a ten-gun, three-masted brig, lay at anchor at Plymouth, England, that December day, 1831. The gangling youth lugged aboard his microscope, his insect nets, and his hopes. As ship's naturalist, the twenty-two-year-old Charles Darwin was outbound on a scientific cruise around the world.

Some bright adventure seemed to lie beyond the cold mist on the western horizon. Darwin was eager for this five-year voyage—after what he considered his five "wasted years" at college.

During his school years, Darwin had given little promise of the scientist he was to become. He had been uncertain about a career. And it is not clear what made him decide finally to become a naturalist.

Perhaps it was something said by a speaker who came to the University of Edinburgh in long hair and wolfskins to lecture excitingly about American wildlife—John James Audubon.

Perhaps Darwin was fascinated by the new idea of studying nature not only in museums and laboratories but in the settings of real and remote worlds. Or perhaps he was led on by the mystery that surrounded living things, like some fog at sea. In an era of great scientific discoveries, little had yet been proved about the kinds and types of creatures on the earth and how they appeared in such variety.

In Darwin's world, most people traced the animals of the earth no farther back in time than the Biblical Noah. And they still believed that the ancestors of all species had been passengers on the flood-bound ark.

The scientists of the 1830s could offer little proof that many species had appeared and others had vanished. Nor could they explain convincingly why or how this had occurred.

Darwin didn't know. And as the *Beagle* floundered out to sea after Christmas, he didn't care, because he was seasick and miserable. He recovered only as the ship crossed the equator on its way toward South America. From the blustery winter, the *Beagle* seemed to head backward in time to the warm days of autumn. In so many other ways, this was a voyage into the past.

For the next three and a half years, the *Beagle*'s company explored the long coasts of the southern continent and the offshore islands.

On August 24, 1833, Darwin suddenly found himself in a lost world. On a windswept Argentine beach, fearfully shunned by the natives, were the bones of nine prehistoric monsters. His gaucho guide watched the elated young Englishman, stroked his chin, and mumbled his amazement. Clearly, some devilish sorcery was responsible for these monstrous skeletons. But how did "Don Carlos" Darwin know all their names?

When Darwin saw the Argentine pampas it seemed to him to be one vast boneyard of ancient beasts. And he was startled to detect in their forms what seemed to be a family resemblance to the living animals of South America.

In his diary he scrawled these words: "The wonderful relationship in the same continent between the dead and the living will, I do not doubt, hereafter throw more light on the appearance of organic beings on our earth, and their disappearance from it, than any other class of facts."

Darwin mentally pieced together the extinct animals represented by the fossils. He compared them in form and structure with the live creatures that he saw around him—huge lizards, odd-shaped mammals, flightless birds, armor-backed crawlers. The dead and the living were "similar and yet so different." The phrase kept recurring to him like the sound of a ship's bell.

In September 1835, the *Beagle* under full sail followed the equator into the open Pacific. The seventh day brought the brig among a group of small islands. These were the Galápagos, burned out volcanic chimneys, rising darkly from the blackened and barren beaches.

On shore Darwin found himself amid strange plants and animals. Only the small birds seemed familiar. The dull-colored finches were like those he knew at home—"similar and yet so different."

Whoever invented the dragon might well have visited the Galápagos, since these islands are the home of its nearest real-life relatives.

Huge swarthy lizards swarm over the islands. Spiny warts and scales cover them from their saw-toothed jaws to their long, curved talons.

To Darwin, they appeared as "imps of darkness." Boldly, he grabbed at one of these lizards as it burrowed in the earth. Instead of breathing fire, the dragon-like creature turned and looked at him in astonishment, Darwin later recalled. "It stared me in the face as much as to say, 'What made you pull my tail?' "

Fierce as they appeared, these lizards were mild and peaceful. Darwin found them reluctant to battle or shed blood. The giant land tortoises were also surprisingly tame, as were so many of the islands' odd-looking creatures.

Darwin prowled about with a gun. But when he approached a large hawk, it refused to budge until he pushed it off its perch with the gun muzzle.

Here, the patterns of living together had become so well established that the animals seemed to have few fears. Each island was the home of species that had developed orderly associations in their dependence on one another. The Galápagos were, in fact, separate communities, or as Darwin called them, "a group of satellites attached to the American continent."

A month of days flew by swiftly as the naturalist toured each of the islands. To his amazement, each was "a little living world within itself." The plants and animals were similar from island to island. And yet there were important differences. The full meaning of these differences came home to Darwin in later years. He wrote:

"I never dreamed that islands, about 50 or 60 miles apart, and most of them in sight of each other, formed of precisely the same rocks, placed under a quite similar climate, rising to a nearly equal height, would have been so differently tenanted."

Darwin had gathered together specimen tortoises from the various islands. All of them seemed very much alike. But he was amazed that an official of the islands could tell at a glance from which island each tortoise had come—as though it carried a label on its back.

Here were types of living things to be found nowhere else on earth. A single tiny island was the only home of entire species of insects, birds, and flowering plants.

The most interesting creatures in this living museum were the little black and brown finches that appeared to be exactly like those Darwin knew in England—except for one thing. Their beaks were different. He counted thirteen different kinds of beak, each belonging to a finch with its own feeding habits, fitting in a special way into its own community. They were later identified as thirteen distinct species.

One species had large, powerful beaks for cracking hard seeds and nuts. Another had chisel-like beaks for gouging in wood. Still others had beaks specialized for cactus-eating, for fly-catching, for sap-sucking.

Some of these finches were plant eaters and others insect eaters. The various species also fed at different levels, from the ground to the treetops.

To Darwin, it seemed that from common ancestors this bewildering assortment of species "had been modified for different ends."

Arrayed before him was a most vivid display of how new living forms may develop under the special conditions of the separate, isolated community. Such striking changes may occur among the inhabitants of some sea island or in a deep mountain valley, among the fish in a land-locked lake, or among the plants in a desert oasis. The living beings are cut off from the main body of members of their species. And in the course of countless generations, these organisms develop variations that harmonize with the special conditions of life. In time, an entire new species may evolve, a species well fitted to a particular role in the interplay of the natural surroundings. Thus the Galápagos birds, amphibians, and reptiles had adapted slowly to ways of life in their communities.

It would be many years before Darwin would fully understand the meaning of what he had seen. But he felt himself being drawn nearer and nearer to "that great mystery of mysteries—the first appearance of new beings on earth."

Some men in previous ages believed that nature advanced from a single series of lower to higher forms of coexisting life. The idea of gradation in living things was proposed by Aristotle in the third century B.C. But in the early nineteenth century, the new concept that all species had evolved from pre-existing ones by an evolutionary process was locked in controversy.

A century before Charles Darwin, the French biologist Georges Buffon had ventured some new ideas on the subject of evolution. A student of his, Jean de Lamarck, had put forward a theory to explain how complex organisms might have developed from simpler ones. It was based, however, on the unproven belief that organisms can transmit to their offspring traits acquired during their lifetime as a result of their own activities.

Charles Darwin was fortunate enough to have close contact with such scientific ideas. One of the main British champions of the theory of evolution was his grandfather, Erasmus Darwin, who had written of living things having a common ancestry.

At Cambridge University, Charles Darwin came into contact with a group of professors who were beginning to challenge some of the age-old dogmas about the scheme of the universe. Darwin also benefited by a lifelong friendship with the geologist Charles Lyell, a brilliant participant in the nineteenth-century debates over natural science. Lyell's explanation of the age and the continuous development of the earth held important clues to the evolution of its living tenants.

These were some of the ideas that Darwin had carried with him aboard the *Beagle*. As he stood watch on the deck of the vessel during the warm tropical nights, he was filled with wonder. On the South American coasts, the structural similarities between the fossils and living animals appeared as a clear record of changing species. On the cluster of lonely Galápagos Islands, he seemed to see evolution at work!

But what was it that brought new varieties, new types, new species into being? What process gave order and direction to the appearance of new forms?

As a boy, Darwin had watched the brilliant flutter of wings from the lofts of British pigeon raisers. What a display of contrasting color and style, of form and flight! In the hope that the breeding of animals might hold some clue to the mystery of how new forms of life arise, Darwin puzzled over pigeons.

Nature had produced a strange member of the pigeon family, called the dodo. Goose-shaped, short-legged, and hook-billed, the dodo now lives only as a delightful character in

Alice in Wonderland, as the species became extinct almost three hundred years ago. Darwin pointed out that this awkward, flightless bird had been a native of a remote island in the Indian Ocean. "It could not have been carried from any other quarter of the world," he said, "nor has it ever been seen or heard of elsewhere."

Some of the odd varieties of pigeons produced by man were studied by Darwin when he returned to England after his voyage on the *Beagle.* Raising pigeons was a popular pastime among British gentlemen. But Darwin went into it not in sport but in scientific earnest. He joined the pigeon-fanciers' clubs, attended the many shows, and set up his own pigeon-breeding pens in an old tree-shaded summerhouse.

The pigeon breeder scrutinizes his charges as they emerge from the egg and as they gradually become full grown. He watches for the traits in which he is interested—color, shape, speed, agility. As Darwin explained: "The breeder has simply to watch for every, even the smallest approach to the desired end, to select such individuals and pair them with the most suitable forms, and so continue with succeeding generations."

In time, he may find his flock marvelously changed. Now there may be brilliant fantails and agile tumblers. Some may have lost all ability to fly, but they are strikingly tinted or skilled at pouting. Still others are carriers or racers.

And yet, as Darwin pointed out, all of this "ornamental poultry" is descended from the homely common rock pigeon. In the wilds this is a creature of the cliffs; in the cities, it makes its home in bridge beams and building cornices.

Darwin studied the art of breeding not only pigeons but also every variety of barnyard animal and field crop, as well as goldfish and silk moths, peacocks and pansies.

"With patience, it is wonderful what man has effected," he

marveled. "He has selected and therefore in one sense made one breed of horses to race and another to pull; he has made sheep with fleece good enough for carpets and other sheep good for broadcloth. He has previously determined how the feathers on a bird's body shall be colored, and how the petals of many flowers shall be streaked or fringed."

The key to it all was the choice made by the breeder as to which animals would be allowed to breed together. As Darwin put it, "I soon perceived that selection was the keystone of man's success in making useful races of animals and plants."

Then the naturalist added: "But how selection could be applied to organisms living in a state of nature remained for some time a mystery to me."

It was a measure of Darwin's integrity as a scientist that he took a quarter of a century before he was willing to publish his conclusions. Meanwhile, he studied facts and shaped ideas. Many of these were fragments, half-formed and developing, like parts of some unborn creature taking shape in the egg.

In the year 1859 Darwin finished the writing of his monumental book *Origin of Species.* His ideas not only violated ancient and widely held religious beliefs, but were in conflict with theories held by many of the foremost scientists of his day.

Some of his friends begged him to change his mind. His publisher trembled when he read Darwin's earth-rocking manuscript. Why not a book on pigeons instead, he pleaded. "After all," said the publisher, "everybody is interested in pigeons."

Darwin had slowly, painstakingly reached his scientific conclusions and nothing could shake him. The mild-mannered Darwin had prepared a bombshell.

5. Fit, Fitter, Fittest

How many things by season season'd are
To their right praise and true perfection!
—SHAKESPEARE, *Merchant of Venice*

Darwin's *Origin of Species* had an explosive impact on the world at large. It also shattered the calm of his own countryside and the quiet of his study.

Darwin was praised as the man who had brought about a revolution in the sciences of life "by the mere force of truth and fact." He was also condemned as "the most dangerous man in England."

A scientific idea as powerful as Darwin's seldom remains the property of scientists alone. Evolution became a bitterly debated topic among people everywhere. In various ways each sought to apply and interpret the broad principles of life set out in Darwin's *Origin of Species* and the half-dozen scientific books that followed.

One English lady was appalled that evolution might link her with some rather low-browed ancestors. "Man descended from apes?" she gasped. "Oh, no, that can't be true. But if it is, let us pray that it may not become generally known."

Darwin, of course, never said that men were descended from apes. He pointed out that earlier forms of life had given rise to the great number of species that we know today, including man. And modern research has confirmed that man could not have evolved directly from any other present-day species.

In more than a hundred years since the publication of *Origin of Species*, the basic ideas that Darwin presented have remained valid. These ideas not only transformed the science of biology but also laid the basis for new branches of the science, including the study of ecology.

The questions that he left unanswered have prodded several generations of biologists since his time. But Darwin's conclusions were so broad that they left room for new scientific findings. Not until many years after his death was the truth disclosed about how traits are passed on through an ancestral heritage. And still more years of research were needed in order to explain the variations in living things which, in Darwin's words, "can not be accounted for by inheritance from either parent or from some remote ancestor."

What Darwin studied was the way organisms tend to vary in form from one another. As the biologist observed, the newborn of every species appear similar and yet are not identical. They differ as do leaves of the same tree or kittens of the same litter or peas in a pod.

These variations are random and unpredictable. Some of the variations may disappear with the death of the individual organism. But others are passed on from one generation to the next, and it is these inherited variations that are involved in the process of evolution.

Another tendency in nature which Darwin pondered was that not all the creatures born will survive. For example, an oyster can produce more than a hundred million eggs in a single spawning. But some never hatch, some die at birth, and others perish in immature stages. Comparatively few manage to reach adulthood. And an even smaller number will have offspring.

Both trends in nature—the variations in individuals and the survival of the few—together form the basis for the process of evolution. Thus out of any population the organisms with those variations well fitted to their environment will tend to survive, and survive *longer*. These are the individuals that will have offspring, and tend to have *more* offspring. If these favored individuals can pass their desirable traits on to their offspring, then the new generations will also be favored.

The picture Darwin drew in his *Origin of Species* was that of nature checking daily and hourly each individual of every species for those variations that makes it better suited for life in a particular environment. He described this process as natural selection.

In the stock pen, it is the breeder who selects. In the wild, it is nature that selects.

Under the controlled conditions of his farm, the animal breeder can achieve changes rapidly, but natural selection works slowly across the vastness of time and through the appearance of countless generations. Slowly, by imperceptible steps, tiny variations keep building to form new species.

Darwin emphasized that natural selection is a process of matching the living organism with its own conditions of life. He concluded: "Those individuals are preserved, whether in their egg or seed or in their mature state, which are best adapted to the place they fill in nature."

The biologist was struck with the way life favors those organisms which, over many generations, have fitted into the new opportunities offered by the environment. For it was such creatures, marvelously adapted, that Darwin had observed in the Galápagos Islands.

In the complete absence of woodpeckers on the Galápagos Islands, one species of finch developed the ability to gouge wood. It does not have the long chisel bill and sticky tongue of familiar woodpecker species. But its beak is strong enough to excavate cracks, and it uses a spine from a cactus plant as a tool to dig deeply into the tree-bark crevices and pry out the worms on which it feeds.

Special adaptive structures are to be found everywhere in nature. Some, like the fins of a fish or the wings of a bird, may not seem remarkable because they are as familiar as the human hand, which itself is wonderfully formed. But every animal has bodily features that have been perfected in eons of evolution to cope with its way of life.

In turbulent waters, some marine animals have developed organs that serve as suction cups to keep them from being washed away. The sure-footed mountain goat is equipped in body to climb hazardous cliffs and to jump from one crag to another. Numerous plants and animals of the desert are adapted for the saving of every drop of water. The paws of the polar bear have hairy pads that enable it to walk on the arctic ice floes.

Such bodily features are not merely well-formed structures. They are adaptations to a specific set of conditions. And if they give a plant or an animal a grip on life it is because the adaptations match the actual, current conditions of its existence.

Organisms adapt slowly and over many generations to certain surroundings, to native habitats. And once these creatures are well adapted, they tend to remain where they are best suited to the setting. This is the arrangement in nature that seems to put creatures in the expected places.

Some species are found only in the dry heights and others near the damp marsh. Some thrive on the sunny side of the hill and others in the shadows. One species invariably chooses the calm pond rather than the running stream. Some animals seek cultivated lands close to mankind, while others need the dense foliage of the virgin forest.

Patterns of adaptation have prepared organisms for a certain style of living which has benefits for them. In some ancient age, the division of labor probably appeared in its simplest form among some primitive ancestors of present-day ants. Since this social way of life was an advantage to the survival of the species, the behavior became fixed in the evolution of ant societies—just as social patterns developed in the evolution of so many other species.

Ants have been called "the mankind of the insect world" because their social lives are so highly organized. The anthill is an amazingly orderly workplace, where the routine duties are divided up among various groups. This social insect is enormously successful and its species carry on their remarkable activity in almost every part of the world.

Some ants are "slaveholders." They invade other species and carry off the immature insects. When they become adults, these "slaves" work for their captors, securing their food and taking care of the nest and the offspring of their "masters."

There are harvester ants that collect seeds and store them in their nests. The leaf-cutter ants carry on a kind of farming, preparing an underground bed of leaves, seeding it with the spores of mushrooms, and eating the crop.

Many adaptations of plants and animals protect them against predators. Some are poisonous to eat. Others are bad-smelling or bad-tasting.

Charles Darwin, who in his youth collected beetles, was startled one day to find three rare specimens at once. Eager to capture all three, he grabbed one in each hand and popped another into his mouth.

"Alas, it ejected some intensely acrid fluid," he later recalled, "which burnt my tongue so that I was forced to spit the beetle out, which was lost, as well as the third one."

Other adaptations for safety occur in the appearance of certain creatures. Predators of the sea often miss their prey because the smaller fish they feed on are matched in color against their backgrounds, whether seen from below or above.

The willow ptarmigan, the state bird of Alaska, varies with the changing colors of its surroundings. Mottled during the summer and early fall to match the foliage, the ptarmigan turns white in the snow season.

While the process of evolution often results in organisms' becoming different, there are other adaptations which make them more similar in appearance. The monarch butterfly with its conspicuous markings has an odor and taste repellent to birds. Several other butterflies, including the viceroy, have developed color patterns like those of the monarch, a resemblance that makes birds shun them as prey.

Still another example is that of four types of animal, each of which closely resembles a leaf so that it escapes the notice of its predators. One is a fish, another is a lizard, a third is a butterfly, and the fourth a grasshopper.

One of the important adaptations to the hazards of life is the rate at which a species reproduces. Clearly, a species must be able to produce a suitable number of offspring if it is to survive as a species. Some reproduce thousands at once. Others have offspring only one by one. And yet these reproduction rates generally tend to keep species either from overrunning the earth or from being exterminated.

Predators eat a great many small plant eaters in a lifetime. Of the two types, the plant eaters tend to have a higher reproduction rate. For example, small rats and mice have larger litters at shorter intervals than do the foxes, owls, snakes, and hawks that feed on them.

At times a species will be confronted with a new and supreme challenge to its ability to adapt. During World War II, the common housefly faced such a time of trial. An insecticide called DDT was discovered which in certain doses proved to be fatal to the housefly. DDT was used against these insects throughout the world. However, by the year 1947, it was clear that, while flies were destroyed in huge numbers, some strains had developed a resistance to DDT. In subsequent generations of houseflies, the resistance to the poison has become more widespread.

The final test of adaptation is in its life-and-death value. When a species has evolved in such a way that it is fitted to meet a constantly changing environment, the individual members of that species have a better chance of surviving. In this sense, life favors birds that can migrate when their food becomes scarce. And plants which can enlist mammals or insects, birds or winds, to distribute their seeds have increased their chances for offspring.

The pattern of survival selects fleetness in an antelope and keen eyesight in a hawk. It favors a rabbit species with a coat that turns white during the snow season and a rodent species that can hibernate during the winter.

The value of adaptation may be seen in the deceptive dappled coloration of the deer fawn at the precise time of life when it requires the most protection from its predators. It is revealed in the ability of the emperor penguin to hold its single egg on the tops of its feet, pressed under a fold of abdominal skin that provides warmth against the icy temperatures of the Antarctic winter. It is exhibited in the ability of a Galápagos finch to live like a woodpecker in an area of the world where no woodpeckers exist.

Such adaptations are not at all changes that organisms make *in order to* survive. They survive *because* their species is adapted to meet the changing conditions of their lives.

There is a well-known nursery rhyme that sings the praises of a married couple who found a pattern for living in harmony:

> Jack Sprat could eat no fat,
> His wife could eat no lean,
> And so between them both, you see,
> They licked the platter clean.

The happy arrangement of the civilized Sprats may also be found in the wild. Many different animals get along fine together—mainly because each has its own distinct eating habits.

In nature, the most successful types of plants and animals are those able to lodge themselves in a livable situation. These species are adapted to a way of life, to a particular place among living and nonliving things.

Each fits into its position, its nook, its niche. The fact is that each species must have a niche of its own—if it is to survive.

According to an ancient Chinese saying, "one hill cannot shelter two tigers." Nor can two species occupy the same niche in the same community.

The term "niche," as used by the ecologist, is actually more than a place, more than a way of achieving food or safety. It encompasses also the nesting habits of a species and its manner of reproduction. An ecological niche also includes the responses of living organisms to the world around them—their relationships to such nonliving features as temperature, moisture, climate, and terrain.

Biologists who studied the insects that live in pine trees found twenty species. Five of them live on different types of pine foliage; three eat buds; three feed on twigs, two on pulp wood, two on roots, one on bark, and the remainder on the layers just below the bark.

The variety of niches that exist in nature may be seen in a forest habitat, some Logtown community. Here two groups of small mammals may appear to be rivals for the same food—except that one group seeks its prey at night while the other forages only during the day.

In the southern woodlands of the United States, John James Audubon found half a dozen species of woodpeckers, sometimes living in the same part of the forest. Although they all ate insects from the bark of trees, Audubon observed that there were marked differences in how each species went about its feeding. He also noted how the woodpecker species differed in their nesting habits. Among them, they used all the various opportunities available to them because of their ability to gouge a home in wood.

As each species confines itself to its own niche, it insures its food, its safety, its way of life. It also avoids harmful competition with other species.

In Logtown, species have niches that vary in time and in space. Some species winter in this community. Others occupy niches that include the habit of migrating or hibernating during the season when food is scarce.

On the forest floor, the woodland crocus blooms in the early spring—before the leaves of the shade trees cut off the sunlight. The gentian blooms in autumn, after many of the tree leaves have fallen.

The Logtown beetles feed at different levels. Some burrow underground. Others grub in a tree trunk. One species is found only on the low branches, and another lives on the high leaves. As for the trees and shrubs, they grow to different heights in keeping with their varied needs for sunlight, some thriving only in bright light and others only in shade.

If the soil were glass we could see the roots below the surface—all at different levels, so that there is the least possible rivalry for water and nourishment.

The niche is the style of living by which a species fits into its total environment. Any habitat on earth is composed of many such niches, which tend to be more numerous in the tropical rain forests and the warm seas than in the deserts or frozen wastelands.

Species that are adapted to similar niches located in various regions of the world are not necessarily similar in body structure. Darwin studied the animals of the South American pampas, where the llama and the guanaco hold the grass-eating niches. As the naturalist sailed westward on the *Beagle* to Australia, he found that the same niches there are occupied by the marsupial kangaroos and bandicoots. In Africa, these niches are filled by zebras and gazelles. On the western plains of America, bison and pronghorns once predominated in the grazing niches. Man has for the most part substituted in these niches his domesticated species of cattle and sheep.

At times, one or more niches in a habitat become vacant. Then one species may, in the slow course of evolutionary change, branch out in response to an abundant and unexploited food supply.

On the Galápagos Islands, Darwin's finches had spread into niches which might otherwise have been filled by other kinds of birds. The islands probably would not have been able to support large numbers of finches, all seeking the same food. But instead of competing with one another, the finches developed a great variety of adaptations. By the process of natural selection, these groups of finches that became adapted in the direction of unfilled niches were preserved.

Natural selection explains how organisms achieved their characteristic forms. And the ecological niche is the way of life to which organisms are fitted by evolutionary changes. Evolving organisms adapt to a niche. They adapt to each other. They adapt to a community.

In the natural community may be found the meaning of events, the reasons for the changing forms of life, the design of growth and movement, adaptation and survival—and the very patterns by which living beings have developed on earth.

In the final paragraphs of *Origin of Species*, Charles Darwin described such a natural community as "a tangled bank clothed with plants of many kinds, with birds singing in the bushes, with various insects flitting about, and with worms crawling through the damp earth. . . ."

In such a scene, the living species appear against their environmental background. Each performs in its own niche. It is like some stage play where the characters appear and disappear. Some species are favored and others emerge briefly, struggle for life, and vanish. At times, the actors change roles. Some performers may be missing and others take their places.

The stage is the natural community. This is the setting in which the timeless pageant is acted out.

Darwin described how dependent these organisms are on one another. They are so varied—and yet they have developed in the course of evolution from a few simple forms, or from only one. The great naturalist found a grandeur in this view of life.

"Whilst this planet has gone cycling on according to the fixed laws of gravity," Darwin wrote, "from so simple a beginning endless forms most beautiful and most wonderful have been, and are being, evolved."

6. The Orderly Wilderness

There was an Old Man with a beard,
Who said, "It is just as I feared!—
Two Owls and a Hen,
Four Larks and a Wren
Have all built their nests in my beard."

—EDWARD LEAR

Lichens are a curious group of plants found in a great variety of places almost everywhere on the earth's land surfaces.

Each species is a combination of two entirely different plants, an alga and a fungus that are mutually dependent on each other. The green alga provides food for the colorless fungus and, in return, the fungus provides the alga with water absorbed by its supporting structures. Because of this peculiar partnership, lichens can thrive on bare rock and in other environments too harsh and discouraging for other vegetation.

One type of lichen that hangs from the branches of trees

is called old man's beard. Out of the fibers of this mossy drapery the parula warbler fashions its nest. This species of warbler is one of the smallest songbirds of the northeastern United States, and ranges only where it can find the old man's beard lichen.

Living things benefit from living together. In some cases, their very existence hinges on how well they are adapted to one another. Some plants and animals have developed parts that fit each other like lock and key.

In our best social behavior, we often "say it with flowers." Most flowers are, in fact, naturally social. The evolution of wildflowers is a brilliant example of how organisms have adapted to each other.

Flowering plants first developed in the age of dinosaurs and flying reptiles. Their kind appeared on this planet some 150 million years ago, long before the time of man. Earlier types of vegetation reproduced by means of naked seeds, exposed on the scales of cones. Their pollen grains and seeds were usually distributed by the winds.

By the process of natural selection, a new form evolved. Its secret was in its encased seed. Once this flowering plant was fertilized, its new promise of life was enclosed in a hardy seed packed with nutrients.

To many of the higher types of seed plants came outside help from insects and birds, some bats and other mammals. Drawn by the fragrant flowers, by the sweet nectar and brilliant colors, they cross-pollinated many of the flowering plants. From that time on, these plants were a dazzling social success, a new form selected by nature to survive and flourish.

The blossoming species are enormously diverse, specialized, and successful. They attract pollinating partners of their own and cover the planet with their beauty. There are bee and moth flowers, beetle and bird flowers, bat and butterfly flowers. Among the showiest and most sweetly scented are those pollinated by insects.

In the year 1858, Charles Darwin received a rare star-shaped orchid from a botanist friend exploring in Madagascar. Darwin marveled at its form, noting that its pollen lay in the bottom of a nectar tube almost a foot long.

If this species was ever to reproduce, Darwin argued, it must be with the help of some unknown creature that is able to draw the pollen from the deep well of the orchid.

Darwin's fellow biologists were skeptical. Then one day a letter from Madagascar brought the news that an orchid-pollinating moth had been found—with a foot-long proboscis.

In southwestern United States, evolution has produced a similar partnership between the yucca plant and a small moth. The yucca flower is shaped in such a peculiar way that it can be fertilized only by means of the specialized mouth parts of the *Pronuba* moth. In turn, the seed pod of the yucca plant provides the nest in which the eggs of this moth develop. When the moth larvae appear, they feed on some of the seeds, but an adequate supply of seeds remains to insure offspring for the yucca plant.

Darwin pointed out, "If insects had not been developed on the face of the earth, our plants would not have been decked with beautiful flowers, but would have produced such poor flowers as we see on our fir, oak, nut, and ash trees, or grasses, spinach, docks, and nettles, which are all fertilized through the agency of the wind."

Studies of the evolution of insects and of flowering plants show that the development of both went hand in hand. To some degree, each adapted to the other, to form many new types. In a similar way, the development of the structure of many species can be understood only as they are related to the other organisms with which they customarily live.

The mistletoe is a parasitic shrub adapted to receive all kinds of assistance. It is pollinated by insects, distributes its seeds by means of birds that eat its berries, and reaches the sunlight by climbing upward on the trunks of certain trees.

The health of some fishes is protected by other fishes and marine animals that are specialized in "cleaning." This form of mutual aid was revealed in recent ecological studies off the southern coasts of the United States. Small kelp perch, for example, are visited by larger fish, which do not prey upon them. The perch enjoy safety and an opportunity for feeding while they clean the parasites and decayed matter from the bodies of larger fish.

A stable relationship among different species arises only in the course of a great many generations. The town in the forest does not happen overnight. Like any man-made town, the natural community has come into being by slow growth. But Logtown residents must take an infinitely longer route—the process of evolution.

The dragonflies darting about the dead log in the woods are the descendants of a long line of transparent-winged beauties. The modern species are only slightly changed from fossil specimens millions of years old.

Toads in this forest community have come a long way both in time and in distance. Not only have they evolved in wondrous ways from earlier forms, but they are also relative newcomers to the North American continent. Their ancestors may have hopped across the land bridge that once connected Asia and Alaska.

The census of Logtown may include a dozen mammals. These are the warm-blooded breast-feeders which have developed

highly organized forms of social life within the community.

Clearly there is some basis in nature for the inhabitants of such a community to live together. And yet, the rivalries within the community often seem too violent for social life to exist at all.

The wild plain is frequently pictured as the setting where the hawk and the snake join in a battle to the death. Stories of the sea depths recount the struggle between the sperm whale and the deadly squid. The tropical savanna is shown as an arena where the lion and the rhino are locked in bloody combat.

The scientist studying nature may also enjoy these stirring tales of "nature in the raw." But the day-to-day pattern he finds is not quite so violent.

In a household where pets are competing with each other

for food and favored treatment, they will fight "like cats and dogs." And in any natural setting, animals will vie against one another for a limited supply of whatever they require for survival.

In nature, there tend to be more mouths to feed than there is easily available food. Other rivalries take place over mates, nesting sites, water, suitable soils. Organisms compete for living space.

Fish choose a territory and defend it. Even plants compete—only a very small number of all the seeds dispersed on a forest floor can find the space and the soil, the moisture and the sunlight, to grow successfully.

The arrival of birds in the spring is usually followed by a period during which each claims ownership of a certain amount of living space.

Often contests between the members of a species are staged when a living area is in the process of change. Animals contend for favorable places in the community. They test each other's strength to seek advantages for themselves.

There is danger and struggle in the wilds, where larger organisms feed on smaller ones. In their dependence on one another, living things display many forms of predatism and parasitism. Large predators stalk and hunt. In immature and young stages, many creatures are easily taken as food, and the aged and disabled seldom survive.

But the wilderness is not a spectacle of continuous warfare between able-bodied predators. The routine in nature will only rarely produce a spine-chilling death struggle between great beasts or groups of beasts evenly matched.

In actual duels between equally powerful beasts, the death blow is often avoided. One fighter or the other proves his superiority quickly and the battle is over. Frequently, there is no blood shed and no blows are struck.

Animals use a wide range of bluff tactics. Howler monkeys, rattlesnakes, screech owls, laughing hyenas are all known by the threatening noises they make. The lion frequently wins his battle with one terrifying roar.

Some moths have bold markings on their wings that resemble eyes. Robins, mandrills, wild turkeys, and cobras frighten their opponents by a display of strong colors or aggressive postures. The skunk has its own nonviolent method of routing a foe.

Wolves often limit their contests within the pack to jaw-snapping, hair-bristling, and ominous growls. Antlered deer duel harmlessly for hours. Many such animals are equipped to destroy one another, but rarely do. For example, competing rattlesnakes that can kill each other with a single venomous bite will usually wrestle with each other until one concedes defeat.

In the Logtown community, spring is the time of greatest rivalry over food. The vegetation has endured the feebleness of the sun and the length of the winter nights. Food supplies are low.

For wintering mammals, the stores of nuts and berries are gone. Hungry offspring are emerging from eggs and cocoons. The hibernating creatures awake famished, and the returning migrators are foraging. This is the time of mating and new birth for many species, and their food needs are greatest.

At such a time the competition is sharpest. And yet the forest community survives. For all its rivalry, spring is, in fact, not a season of death and destruction, but rather of new life and growth.

Each individual of every species strives to live amid its surroundings. In this sense, there is constant struggle to survive.

The desert animals "struggle" to find water. The sapling growing in the forest must "struggle" to find a place in the sun. Clams "struggle" against the ceaseless flogging of the surf.

On the prairie, there is a many-sided "struggle" for the tender grass that involves not only sheep and antelopes, but also rabbits and mice, as well as grasshoppers and crickets.

It was Darwin who pointed out that "the struggle will invariably be most severe between the individuals of the same species, for they frequent the same districts, require the same foods, are exposed to the same dangers."

Numerous experiments have been conducted by ecologists and other biologists on the social behavior of animals. In the laboratory, mice, dogs, and chickens have been observed, to test their reactions toward one another. Many natural conditions have also been studied to learn why animals fight and why it is also possible for groups of creatures to reach a high degree of orderly living.

Although there is no final set of answers, and the full meaning of some results is not yet clear, these experiments do reveal many of the ways that animals seek to avoid conflict.

The patterns in nature seem to show that, when a species can possibly avoid harmful competition with other species, it usually does so. The effort toward survival impels organisms to lead busy and productive lives. There is cooperation as well as competition. And most creatures seem to live in a state of neutrality toward one another.

While frictions occur when animals seek a territory, additional struggle is avoided when the other animals recognize the claim.

Animals which might compete bitterly over a declining food supply often avoid such outbreaks by means of hibernation or migration.

The arrangement of creatures in separate ecological niches has the effect of avoiding conflict and establishing an orderly pattern throughout nature wherever living things are found.

In *The Descent of Man,* Darwin pointed out that "in numberless animal societies, the struggle between separate individuals for the means of existence disappears; struggle is replaced by cooperation."

Two of the boys in Darwin's neighborhood once prepared a little hoax for the kindly naturalist.

They had glued together wings, legs, and pieces of several different insects and asked him to identify "the strange bug we found."

Darwin examined their specimen carefully. At length, he asked, "When you found it, did it make a loud, humming sound?"

"Oh yes," the boys replied eagerly.

"Just as I thought," said Darwin. "It's a humbug!"

Darwin had a delightful sense of humor. But he often became upset at the "humbug" which was passed off in the name of "Darwinism."

Although large numbers of people of his day did not understand *Origin of Species* fully, many found it a revealing guide to life on this planet. Others read into it things that Darwin had never written and meanings he had never intended.

Darwin was himself a mild and modest person. But his was an aggressive and violent age. The England of the time was later described by Prime Minister Benjamin Disraeli as "divided into two nations—the rich and the poor." And the contrast was even greater between wealthy Britons and the millions of black, brown, and yellow colonial peoples who were ruled under the British lion, the symbol of the empire All of the European powers grappled for colonies, but Great Britain took the lion's share.

As Britain fought to hold and extend its empire abroad,

there were many problems at home, as well. These were the stormiest years of Britain's mounting Industrial Revolution.

In this stream of events the *Origin of Species* appeared. In such a time, it was understandable that a new scientific idea such as Darwin's might become caught up in the political and social currents of the day.

Some prominent Britons thought they could see in Darwin's writings a parallel between the patterns of nature and those in nineteenth-century British politics. Even the full title of Darwin's book was misinterpreted in this fashion. On the title page, Darwin had written: "On the Origin of Species by Means of Natural Selection, or the Preservation of Favoured Races in the Struggle for Life."

As the term "race" is used in biology, it refers to a variety that occurs within a species. The race is ordinarily a particular group, living in a distinct climate or region, and developing some variations in body structure which distinguish it from other organisms within the species. Such a race may become the basis for a new species.

Darwin's use of the word "race" had nothing to do with the false theories which attempt to divide mankind into superior and inferior races or to set up a "master race."

One British newspaper said that Darwin had proved that "might makes right." Some writers distorted the meaning of Darwin's emphasis on the struggle for existence in nature. They drew the false conclusions that all of nature, including man, lives by a "law of the jungle," that all are involved in savage rivalries which are won only by the most powerful, that any means to wealth and victory can be justified.

Most unfortunate of all was the misuse and misunderstanding of one phrase that Darwin used—"survival of the fittest." Certainly he had never intended to justify aggressive behavior by empire-builders, militarists, merchants, and industrialists. But the word "fittest" was interpreted to refer to brute strength, both in the wild and in human affairs.

In truth, Darwin's emphasis was on the real secret of survival—the ability of beings to fit into their surroundings. Such adaptations are seen in organisms large and small, in both the forceful and the frail.

In his late years, Charles Darwin sought to clarify the true meaning of the struggle in nature. He tried to correct the false impression that the evolution of life on earth was merely one long record of victor and vanquished. He pointed out that the chief striving of living things is "for the greatest possible fullness and intensity of life." Natural selection is not a destructive force but a creative one.

If all of nature were really in a state of ceaseless warfare, the natural landscape would be one vast battlefield, instead of the setting for the orderly series of thriving natural communities that it is.

If violence were actually the only law of life, the earth would be ruled by a few fierce species. However, the ferocious *Tyrannosaurus* and the saber-toothed tiger have long disappeared. The docile tortoise and the fragile May fly remain.

Darwin revealed how the unfolding of newer and higher forms on earth led eventually to man, the human species—a remarkable being that arose from pre-existing forms.

It might seem that man was ill-prepared for the problems of life as he found them. He was smaller and weaker than many other creatures, without fangs or powerful claws.

He lacked the sharp eyesight of the hawk, the swiftness of the antelope, the keen hearing of the fox. He was not endowed with special organs for burrowing or flying, for swimming or climbing. He was not especially adept at hiding or smelling out food or protecting his young. Compared to most other organisms, he produced only small numbers of offspring, who remained helpless for years and matured very slowly.

How did he pass the test of natural selection? What gave him his power of survival?

His great strength was in the matchless quality of his brain. Born without skills, he could learn an endless variety of them. His brain was a great source of adaptibility.

He had the gift of his community-living forebears—the traits that made him a high type of social animal. Adapted in body to only a narrow range of environments, he could learn to solve countless problems in living. He could fit himself into any environment where life was possible.

7. Man in Command

Be fruitful, and multiply, and replenish the earth, and subdue it; and have dominion over the fish of the sea, and over the fowl of the air, and over every living thing that moveth upon the earth.

—GENESIS

Early man trembled at the flash and thunder overhead, at the might of glaciers and the force of the sea tides. Through his long centuries of savagery, man lived almost like any other animal in the natural community. And yet, the ancient record shows how different he was.

On the walls of limestone caves in France and Spain, early man depicted the wildlife around him. These paintings expressed wonder at the grace of the stag and the grandeur of the bison. In some of the caves spears and other tools were found around the ashes of fires where he sat and planned the hunt with members of his clan. Nearby were the gnawed bones of large animals that a single man could not have brought down alone.

There were also relics of his magic. He tried with charms and idols and whispered chants to gain further control over nature. He planned in order to insure his supplies of game, fruit, berries, and honey. He prepared his defenses against the sudden storm and the wild boar.

Nature appeared to him as some great beast—to be appeased or held at bay. This was man fighting to gain the upper hand. To some extent, these patterns of struggle between man and nature, which arose during the raw dawn of human life on earth, would continue for a million years.

If the human species straightened up from an apelike crouch, it was with a growing sense of confidence. From the beginning, man used his fine brain to cope with his surroundings. He joined in strong social efforts for the assault on nature. He developed the use of tools and fire and speech. He competed with wolves for prey. He was defiant and venturesome, crossing the next river and the next range to find what lay beyond.

Eventually man learned to transmit his thoughts through pictures and symbols and finally through a written language. In place of ineffective magic, he soon found the comforts of religion and the uses of science. He came to believe that he and his kind were chosen to master the earth.

The mammoth that he hunted later vanished as a species. Man survived. Other species, endangered by any great changes in the physical world around them, might adapt to the new conditions through the long, slow process of evolution. But man also had the ability to change himself.

Having no growth of fur on his own body to keep him warm, he used the bear's hide for clothing. He could build a shelter to withstand the turn of the seasons. By cooking food over a fire, in a pot which he fashioned, he added to what was edible. He developed ways to trap fish, to soothe a fever, to make tools of stone, of bronze, and of iron.

In the quietest of his great revolutions, man tamed a few goats, planted the first handfuls of wheat and barley seeds. From that time on, man became involved in a vast effort to mold nature to his will.

This venture is over ten thousand years old. It dates back to the time when men became dissatisfied with their lives as roving hunters and food gatherers, foraging only when hungry and wandering before the wildest winds. They selected a few species as food animals and food crops. From then on, it was man and his chosen species in a struggle against the rest of the natural community.

As a wanderer, man had made few changes in the landscape. He might return again and again to a favored hunting ground. Between times, the living communities that he had visited had time to heal from any damage.

When he began to cultivate the land, man made some sweeping changes. He cut down forests. He changed the content of the soils, drained marshes, and built roads and dams, pastures and towns.

Nature was no match for the man with the torch and the plow, the rifle and the ax. He changed the relationships between the living and the nonliving. He sought constantly for new crops to plant. By selection, he changed the breeds and varieties of what he raised. He revised the numbers and kinds of species living in certain habitats.

Man could enter into almost any kind of natural community. He could live in it. He could often change it. He could sometimes destroy it.

Man could ably adapt to life around him. The rest of the living world was not so well prepared to live with him.

A strange package was shipped from Cincinnati one September day in 1914. Encased in a three-hundred-pound block of ice was a passenger pigeon named Martha, the last member of a magnificent breed.

Audubon described the species: "Their body is formed in an elongated oval, which they steer with a long, well-plumed tail and propel with well-set wings, the muscles of which are very large and powerful for the size of the bird. A bird seen gliding through the woods and close to the observer passes like a thought; and the eye tries in vain to see it again, but the bird is gone."

The passenger pigeon was not some rare creature. In Audubon's day, it was the most numerous of all American birds.

Despite its delicate beauty, the passenger pigeon was widely hunted. In 1813, Audubon described a scene on the banks of the Green River in Kentucky as the birds arrived in great numbers at a favorite haunt.

"As the time of the arrival of the passenger pigeons approached, their foes anxiously prepared to receive them. Some persons were ready with iron pots containing sulphur, others with torches of pine knots; many had poles, and the rest, guns. . . .

"Then the authors of all this devastation began to move among the dead, the dying and the mangled, picking up the pigeons and piling them in heaps. When each man had as many as he could possibly dispose of, the hogs were let loose to feed on the remainder."

Although he was grieved by such conduct, Audubon firmly believed that the passenger pigeons were so plentiful that they would persist as a species and never die out. He was wrong.

Throughout the nineteenth century, they were seen less and less frequently. The last surviving passenger pigeon died in 1914 in the Cincinnati Zoo. Its body was sent in ice to the Smithsonian Institution in Washington, D.C., where it was stuffed and put on display.

In the brief history of the United States, dozens of other species have vanished forever. Scores of others are fading out.

The bald eagle, our national bird, once widespread throughout America, is now gone from many states and threatened with complete extinction.

After California achieved statehood, its residents proudly put the grizzly bear on their state flag. Not long afterward every grizzly bear in the state was gone.

Although it is now plentiful again, the beaver was almost exterminated during the nineteenth century, when its pelt was used to make men's hats. Native egrets, spoonbills, and herons, now rare, were taken for the plumage to decorate ladies' hats. What helped to save these species was a change in the hat styles, decided by the leaders of fashion.

Any species that has come this far down the road of evolution has proven its ability to survive. It has been shaped, adapted, perfected in the course of thousands of generations. It has succeeded biologically where countless others failed.

In many cases a species became extinct because it was unable to adjust or adapt as the world about it changed. It failed in the test of time.

As for the passenger pigeon, it disappeared along with the virgin forests that covered the eastern part of this continent. The coming of the white settlers with their axes and guns marked a change in the environment which this species could not survive.

Bryce Canyon in Utah winds through a maze of limestone cliffs in an area that abounds in natural beauty. It is the home of marmots and mariposa, of porcupines and ponderosa pines.

This land of breathtaking grandeur was named after Ebenezer Bryce, a cattle rancher who abandoned it in sheer disgust. To him, the canyon was merely "a dandy place to lose a cow."

The comment is typical of a hard-headed attitude that in one century transformed the American West. Within a brief period, new species of plants and animals appeared on the Great Plains and the old ones vanished. Sage and bluestem grass were replaced by wheat and corn. The great herds of buffalo and pronghorn gave way to cattle and sheep. Across a vast area, the patterns of nature were rearranged by man in keeping with his needs.

For centuries, the Indians had lived in this region, changing it very little. They were, of course, few in numbers compared to the present-day population. But the Indians lived in simple fashion, taking from nature only what they needed, giving in return their thanks and respect.

Plants and animals were carefully harvested according to the season and the requirements of the tribe. Buffaloes, or bison, were regarded by the Plains Indians as a sacred trust, and when the buffaloes were plentiful, the Indians pledged in their ceremonies to leave other animals in peace. Buffaloes were used not only for fresh and dried meat. The horns, the hides, and the hair were used to make moccasins and ropes, lodge coverings and utensils.

The Indians lived at one with the wilderness around them. In their religious outlook they exalted moderation and shunned waste. They believed that such misfortunes as illness or lack of game were caused by throwing the world of nature out of balance. They did not condemn any living creature because they did not understand its use or see its role in the scheme of nature.

Many of the white men who invaded their lands had a different outlook. They crossed the frontier in search of opportunity. The question they asked about whatever they saw was: "What good is it?" They took the attitude that anything that did not serve their own needs was "useless." Since they were able to sell buffalo skins, the animals were worth more dead than alive.

To the everlasting sorrow of America, the buffaloes vanished by the millions—and often for the worst reasons. Thousands were shot merely for sport from the car windows of the newly built railroads. Many were cleared from the Western ranges by cattlemen. And still more buffaloes were destroyed because they gave sustenance to those Indian tribes that stood in the way of "the winning of the West."

The coming of the white man brought important changes to the Great Plains and to its living communities. The settler brought new plant and animal species and changed the patterns of life. He disturbed the soil with the plow—and sometimes learned that it could never again be set at rest.

Soil can be thought of as a community combining fragmented rock with living and dead organisms. It lies on the land areas of the earth in shallow layers, thinning out to nothing in many regions. Usually it is held in place by growing plants. And if the plants are destroyed, the soil may be quickly carried off by water or wind.

In the Old World, man's heedless treatment of the soil sometimes formed uninhabitable deserts. Lands "flowing with milk and honey" later became barren and lifeless. Some of these patterns were repeated in the New World. Rich grasslands were destroyed on America's western plains and became dust-filled wastelands.

In the United States, a cropland area bigger in size than the entire state of Nebraska was abandoned because of soil erosion. The rootless topsoil took the water route from rut to gully, from stream to river—out to the open sea.

America was expanding into a great modern nation. But something was happening to the landscape, to the clear streams and the towering woodlands.

8. Learn and Live

We cannot command nature
except by obeying her.
—FRANCIS BACON

In the days of Audubon and Thoreau, it is said that a squirrel could travel in the trees overhead from the Atlantic to the Mississippi without touching ground.

Great virgin forests crowned America. And when they began to disappear, many Americans were roused to anger and action. What followed at the beginning of the twentieth century was the formation of the conservation movement. This was a gathering of many leaders in public and private life, as well as ordinary citizens, who were outraged and heartsick by what they saw happening to this country's natural bounty and beauty.

Some responded most strongly to the "cut-and-get-out" misuse of the woodlands. Some protested the use of the clear streams as sewage systems. Others were saddened at the way huge livestock herds were being driven across the grass ranges in a manner that left nothing but wasteland. And still others felt that the methods used in breaking in on the stored wealth of the earth disregarded the future fuel and mineral needs of America.

There were portions of this nation that were beginning to take on the appearance of some barren landscape on the moon. Badlands were being created by unwise forms of farming. Ugly scars of earth were upheaved by strip mining. Poisonous fumes from smelters left blackened areas where nothing would grow.

Most disturbing was the strong response by the natural world to some of man's heedless actions. Disaster might result from riding roughshod over the landscape. It could come with the swiftness of a flash flood or the slow pace of the creeping dust that choked the land.

The conservation groups began to educate the people across America. They showed that the country no longer had resources to waste. They made it clear that, for all its abundance, there was a limit to what nature could offer. Somewhere there was an end to the quantities of oil and white oak, of bison and passenger pigeons.

The damage was being done, conservationists believed, not by evil and destructive men. Instead, they felt that many of the problems could be overcome through education in better and more scientific methods. They sought to prove to those who made their living from the land that it is not wise or practical to be short-sighted in dealing with nature.

The conservation movement included dozens of different organizations. Some were most interested in preserving natural resources. Others represented the interests of hunters and fishermen. Still others sought to improve the techniques of ranching and farming.

However, some conservation groups worked mainly to preserve the living beauty of nature, to keep portions of the natural community wild and free. They were more interested in what is wondrous than in what is profitable.

In the year 1858, Henry David Thoreau sounded the plea which later supporters of conservation were able to bring to reality in the vast network of American parks and wildlife areas. Thoreau called for "national preserves, in which the bear and the panther . . . may still exist, and not be civilized off the face of the earth—not for idle sport or food, but for inspiration and our own true education."

During the first half of this century, the conservation movement made great strides. This time span covers the period from the important conservation laws sponsored by President Theodore Roosevelt to some of the highest achievements during the administration of President Franklin Delano Roosevelt.

The attitude of the latter Roosevelt is best shown by an incident in 1941. The United States Army was planning to set up a field artillery range at Henry Lake, Utah. The lake was the home of the trumpeter swan, a species which had become rare and in danger of extinction.

After protests by conservation groups, the President instructed the Secretary of War to change his plans. "The verdict is for the trumpeter swan and against the Army," said Roosevelt's memo. "The Army must find a different nesting place."

The conservation movement grew and its problems became more complex. Its methods were often those of trial and error, trying almost everything and making painful errors.

The tragedy of the deer on Arizona's Kaibab Plateau was a dramatic example. In the Kaibab area, well-meaning people set about "helping" the deer herd. Their idea was to launch a campaign to kill off some of the predators that feed on deer, particularly the wolves, cougars, and coyotes. As a result the deer herd expanded from four thousand in 1906 to a hundred thousand in 1931.

The natural community did not, however, contain enough food for the increased number of deer. In the years that followed, the area was overbrowsed and much of the vegetation and crops damaged or destroyed by hungry deer. The tragic result was that deer died of starvation by the thousands.

Better answers to conservation problems seemed to lie in a deeper understanding of the complex relationships in nature. More and more, those interested in conserving the natural resources turned to the scientists for answers. Gradually, scientific methods were developed for managing wildlife, conserving underground fuels and minerals, maintaining streams and lakes, raising food and fiber crops.

When man plants a field or fences a pasture, he takes a single species and makes it supreme, often in an area where it never existed before.

Such a change hardly can be made without bringing some vigorous response from nature. And it is the farmer who finds himself in the middle of an age-old struggle, serving mankind's food needs and keeping the rest of nature on the far side of the fence.

For all of his difficulties, the American farmer more than fulfilled his role as a producer. But he was to learn again and again what may happen in an area where a rich variety of living things is replaced by a single crop.

Across America's cotton belt, communities that depended on the one crop have repeatedly faced disaster. The cotton plant is the favored food of the boll weevil, a tiny beetle that attacks this crop with vigor and thoroughness, year after year.

After perilous decades of uncertain cotton farming, the town of Enterprise, Alabama, decided to change its entire way of living. Other crops and industries were established The town recovered, prospered, and vowed it would never return to a one-crop system. In 1910, the townspeople erected a statue to the beetle that had shown them their error. The statue still bears a plaque inscribed: "In profound appreciation of the boll weevil."

In many farming communities, however, food growers continue the ceaseless and baffling task of keeping invaders in check. Powerful equipment and chemicals have been devised to cope with them. Often the solution is only temporary—or it may strike back in unexpected ways.

The bewildered farmer has set poisoned traps and caught his own livestock. He has drenched areas with insect sprays and contaminated his own cranberries. He has spread weed-killers, which were rainwashed into his pond, destroying his fish.

Often the poisons have entered into food chains with far-reaching and dismaying results. In some areas, the insecticides have poisoned the songbirds and muted the morning. A farmer may unwittingly destroy the insect-eating birds on his farm. He may then find his crops harvested by the insects, which are no longer under control.

In the year 1859, the growing of Irish potatoes was being introduced on farms across the United States. A small yellow-and-black-striped beetle then lived in obscurity in the Rocky Mountains of Colorado. It was so obscure that it did not

even have a popular name. But it soon achieved notoriety.

This ten-striped beetle advanced into every area where the potato was being grown, stripping the leaves from each plant and destroying the crop. From that time until now, potato farmers have been in a continuous and often losing battle with this insect.

Some harassed farmers have dubbed it the arithmetic bug since it "adds to the misery, subtracts from the harvest, and multiplies like the dickens." Many viewed the potato beetle simply as a creature that acquired a dislike for farmers and a taste for potatoes.

The biologists have a different view. They know the potato beetle as an insect that was adapted to live on the buffalo bur, a plant closely related to the potato. And when the buffalo-bur beetle found the potato, it had a food supply much to its liking.

Scientific explanations are not always so simple. Nor is finding the explanation quite the same as finding the solution to the problem. Nevertheless the ecological method points toward the orderly flowing patterns in nature. And often the solution for man is to find some way of working with the stream of life instead of going against it.

The French farmer in the rolling valleys of the Rhone makes a staircase of ponds. By arranging small dikes and dams, he carries on a plan of alternate water farming and land farming.

In his ponds he raises fish and waterfowl for several seasons. When the ponds are drained out, there is a fertile bed for wheat and barley. After several grain crops have left their rich stubble after the harvest, the fields are flooded again for the water crops.

The modern American farmer has the equipment with which to clear off the tangled patches of shrubbery that grow wild on the far edges of his field. But many have learned sound reasons why these bordering natural communities should remain untouched. The underbrush is the cover for a few foxes that keep the mouse and rabbit population in check. The wild thicket is the nesting place of birds, each of which eats hundreds of insects daily and carries more back to hungry nestlings. The weed patch is the home of the wild bees that pollinate the clover crop.

Thus, despite their name, which signifies undesirable plants, even weeds have their place in the over-all pattern of nature. In fact, some of them have a popularity of their own. The goldenrod is considered a weed, and yet it is the official blossom of three states—Kentucky, Alabama, and Nebraska. The bluebonnet is called a weed almost everywhere—except in Texas, where it is the beloved state flower.

The evening primrose and the sunflower are weeds to those who do not appreciate their beauty, and the cattail is a weed to anyone who does not love the marshland. The fennel may be a weed to those who do not know how to season a sauce with its flavor.

A weed is any plant that happens to be "in the wrong place at the wrong time," in the farmer's narrow view. Perhaps a rose is a weed—if it is growing in a cornfield.

An open field seems to be an open invitation to plants and animals. The farmer sees the weeds as wild-growing enemies of his crops. To the biologist the weed is a hardy plant species with an unusually strong grip on life. Cultivated plants are beset by insects and animals that chew, suck, cut, and tear at their tissues, and the food-grower fights them as pests. The ecologist recognizes these so-called pests as would-be members of the natural community, trying to move into—or to move back into—an area their species once occupied.

In two well-known fables the Pied Piper rid Hamlin town of rats and Saint Patrick drove the snakes out of Ireland. In reality the problems of dealing with harmful species are seldom that simple. However, the ecologist can sometimes offer a novel solution.

In 1957 a group of scientists tackled a problem in ecology posed by baffled Florida cattlemen. The problem was the screwworm fly, an insect deadly to livestock.

The scientists looked for an answer that lay somewhere in the behavioral patterns of the insect itself. They studied its life cycle, its mating habits, its relation to other organisms, its reaction to temperature and climate, its migrations, its method of laying eggs in the open wounds of its victims.

A plan was worked out in the laboratory and carefully tested in field experiments. It was designed to reach a single target—the screwworm fly—and to leave the rest of the ecological structure relatively undisturbed. No poisons which could be passed on to other organisms would be used. And the insect could not possibly adapt to the new conditions which they meant to impose.

The plan consisted in distributing large numbers of screwworm flies. These, however, would be insects made sterile in the laboratory and unable to produce offspring.

Some of the cattlemen had their doubts. But their previous efforts with chemical sprays had brought them nothing but grief. They were ready to try anything.

That winter, twenty small airplanes began infesting the state of Florida each week with fifty million additional screwworm flies—flies that could never become parents.

As the healthy flies mated with the sterile ones, the new generations of flies gradually came to a dead end. Within a period of seventeen months, the menace of the screwworm fly had ceased to endanger the grazing herds of cattle in Florida.

This is an example of what sometimes can be done when a problem is seen through the eyes of the scientist. In the science of ecology, men and women investigate what may happen when one food-chain link, one species, is eliminated—or when a brand new one is introduced.

Some of the plant and animal wildlife that Americans enjoy are not "natives" at all. Some species, like the cattle egret,

made their own way from the old world to the new. Others deliberately brought to the United States include soybeans, avocadoes, Dutch tulips, Persian melons, Scotch pine, Egyptian cotton.

Many transplanted species survived only under human care. Some were imported and turned loose to grow wild. The pheasant was brought in from China, the so-called Kentucky bluegrass is a species native to Europe, and the common sparrow is English in origin.

The ecologist can explain how the successful species fitted

nicely into an American niche. He can show why these species survived here, and without causing any serious upset in the existing patterns of life. The ecologist also reveals why man's efforts to rearrange nature do not always turn out so well.

Back in 1844, a water hyacinth was brought into Louisiana to add to the beauty of the scenery. Since then, this fast-growing plant has spread throughout several Southern states, causing millions of dollars' worth of damage. Each year, the water hyacinth clogs the channels of the rivers and streams, making them impassable.

In 1872 the mongoose was imported to the West Indies from India in an effort to curb the rats and their raids on the sugar cane. At first, the plan was somewhat successful. But it proved to be a foolish hope that this animal could be kept on a strict diet of rats. The mongoose went on to destroy waterfowl, ground-nesting birds, and even barnyard animals. Today the people of the West Indies have not only a rat problem but a mongoose problem as well.

In the natural community, the numbers of each species are usually held in some kind of loose balance. Something happens when man thoughtlessly alters the natural arrangement to suit himself. The pattern often turns wild. There is sudden chaos in place of the order established by nature through the long process of evolution.

A little over a hundred years ago, an Australian named Thomas Austin ordered some live rabbits from England. They arrived by clipper ship and were turned loose. Previously unknown on that continent, the rabbits took avidly to Australian life.

The rabbit population grew by leaps and bounds. Within fifty years, their numbers had soared to two billion—about three hundred rabbits for every human being on the continent.

The rabbits denuded the grassland and drank the water holes dry. They fed greedily on such crops as alfalfa and cabbage, corn and clover. They devoured the food of the sheep herds and of the human population as well.

Even bringing in foxes failed to help. The foxes seemed to prefer lambs to rabbits. Weasels and ferrets were imported. They killed few rabbits and instead raided the chicken houses.

In desperation, the Australians finally resorted to poisons and then to spreading a virus disease which has a deadly effect on rabbits. In recent years, however, there have been growing reports of certain new strains of rabbits which are able to resist the poison and are immune to the disease. By the process of natural selection, hardy new varieties have appeared. Australians have new cause for worry about the future of their war with the rabbits.

When Thomas Austin released those rabbits because he wanted rabbits to hunt, he had no idea what he had begun. He had no notion of what may happen among rabbits in a setting without the foxes which keep the rabbit population in check in other countries. He didn't know that he would disrupt the long-existing food chains of the Australian countryside. He was unaware that he might be upsetting the natural communities. He didn't realize that the rabbits would find in Australia a large niche in which they could thrive.

The science of ecology might have pointed to some of these hazards. But in the middle of the nineteenth century, ecology did not exist as a science or even as a word. There were only the foundations of ecology being laid by men like Charles Darwin.

9. No Place Like Oikos

No man is an island, entire of itself; every man is a piece of the continent, a part of the main; if a clod be washed away by the sea, Europe is the less, as well as if a promontory were, as well as if a manor of thy friends or of thine own were . . . .
—JOHN DONNE, *Devotions*

Great men seem to free us from a narrow and short-sighted view of things.

Columbus sailed boldly toward the riddle beyond the rim of the sea. Galileo extended man's vision to the distant stars.

Charles Darwin gave life on earth its true dimension of time. His measuring units were not years but generations, thousands of them. And after Darwin, man could at last look back and see how far the road of evolution stretched behind him.

Darwin also disclosed the unity of all life on the planet by showing how organisms relate to one another. Out of Darwin's insight came a new era in biology—and the beginnings of the science of ecology.

In the latter half of the nineteenth century, the life sciences moved ahead rapidly. During this period it was proved that organisms come only from other living organisms. The cell theory was expanded to explain the structure of all living things. The germ theory explained the cause of many diseases and revealed parasitic life in its smallest forms.

In this setting of discovery, the science of ecology began its own special approach to life. Ecology is rooted in the truth that neither man nor any species can live alone. And its chief concern is with the ways of living together.

Living beings are dependent on one another, linked by food chains. They are joined by cycles which circulate the energy and the chemical substances needed for life. Species act as a check on one another, so that populations are kept within livable limits. Species tend to find the niches in which they can live satisfactorily. And they can sometimes adapt to new niches when and where they are available.

These are some of the principles with which the ecologist works. He studies life within the structure of the living community. Just as one cell is a unit within a multi-celled organism, so is a single community a unit of nature. The community can exist in an area as small as a drop of pond water or a bit of soil, or in a territory as wide as the earth. It is always possible to draw a larger circle around a smaller one. Similarly, the community can always be considered not only as an individual unit but also as a part of a larger unit.

Today, the science of ecology, still very young, offers much to the person who will enter its many fields of search and service. It is no longer possible to find new continents in sailing ships, but the undiscovered worlds of ecology remain.

One may travel around the world, as Darwin did or like Thoreau, stay close to home.

To Thoreau, there were a thousand fascinating worlds of nature right in his own community. "I have traveled widely around Concord," he once said.

The intricate patterns of ecology may be traced in a wood-lot or a millpond. The experiments of ecology can be home-made in a backyard garden, in a miniature zoo, in a classroom aquarium. Countless living communities may be studied without any need to capture, kill, or collect.

There are mysteries in the marsh. There are the strange and special ecologies of whales and wasps, of insect-eating plants and slave-keeping ants. There is the desert, with its moisture-holding plants and dry-skinned animals that seem to come alive only after the blazing sun has burned itself down on the horizon. There are the fascinating surface waters of the sea, where plant and animal life shimmers in the night—a world that intrigued young Darwin as he dragged a net from the stern of the *Beagle.*

While other branches of biology go deeply into the details of life processes, ecology offers a broader, far-ranging view. Other biologists reduce living matter to smaller and smaller fragments for study, but ecologists are concerned with the larger and more complex levels of organized living.

In dealing with the way that individuals and groups react to one another and to their surroundings, the ecologist is faced with the greatest challenge of all in his attempt to comprehend the role man plays today in changing the environment on a global scale.

Ecology devotes itself to studying, describing, and understanding the total community. This young science is called on increasingly to help *solve* the urgent problems of a man-transformed world.

The handprint of man can be found on almost every landscape. If the result is ugly in some places, it is pleasing in others.

Nature has its way with the land. But there is also man-made beauty in a hedgerow of willows, in a peaceful village, in a patchwork of grain fields and orchards.

Man's works include the rice terraces in the Philippines and the towers of the great cities, the lemon groves reclaimed from the Sahara Desert and the tulip beds that Holland won back from the sea.

Some of man's best efforts are those that blend with nature. And these include the great public parks of America, the sanctuaries for wildlife, and the growing number of areas set aside as wilderness.

"We need the tonic of wildness," Thoreau once wrote, "to wade sometimes in marshes where the bittern and the meadow-hen lurk, and hear the booming of the snipe; to smell the whispering sedge where only some wilder and more solitary fowl builds her nest, and the mink crawls with its belly close to the ground."

These wild areas are where we can learn most about nature. The wilderness is a matchless laboratory. Its value is boundless. This is also where we fulfill the deep human need for a warmer kinship with the creatures and the vegetation with which we share the planet.

And yet, few of us can wander off at will to some woodland Walden where life is primitive and simple. We have new ways of life and will not return to the past.

Modern man is part of a more complex society that has

built new modes of living. The man-made communities grow larger and more remote from the wild world of nature. In building an advancing civilization, man is carried forward to new environments.

Each day brings new inventions and improved technology that modify the conditions of life. But there are a number of unwanted changes that follow in the stream of progress as well.

For example, the air and water of many cities and industrial communities have been fouled and polluted. Dirty streams and lakes are not only ugly but also injurious to health. Foul air is not only unpleasant but poisonous as well.

A thick gray veil hangs over many cities. It carries smoke and fumes, dust and ash. Many of the noxious substances are the products of burning fuels. Some of the most dangerous of all pollutants cannot be seen. They travel invisibly across the globe. Traces of the insect poison DDT have shown up throughout the world, wherever samples of the atmosphere have been analyzed. Radioactive substances, the products of nuclear-bomb tests, have appeared in varying quantities on every continent.

Some of the dangerous substances not only travel in the atmosphere but also enter into food chains. Insecticides have been traced from plants to birds and mammals. Radioactive substances originating in the explosions of nuclear weapons fall out of the atmosphere onto the grass of a cow pasture, and then appear in cow's milk.

Many human ailments can be traced directly or indirectly to contaminated air and water. There may be unknown long-range effects on health as well.

In the record of life on earth, no species has survived in a changing environment for which it was not fitted. Certain plants and animals find it impossible to live in modern cities. Lichens, hardy enough to survive in some of the most difficult environmental conditions on earth, have long been disappearing from industrial areas.

Can such communities be made safe and healthful? Can their residents be assured of the clean air and fresh water that are so essential to human life?

It may require man's highest intelligence to solve such problems. It may take the full resources of the sciences—including the science of ecology.

As a science, ecology has no hard boundaries. It is naturally linked with many neighboring sciences.

The work of ecologists brings them into contact with the scientists who study the land and the sea and the climates of the earth. They share ideas with biologists who probe the structure and behavior and development of organisms.

In turn, other scientists have found great value in the viewpoint of ecology. For example, medical scientists see the importance of applying the ecological approach to the problems of disease and health. Typhus carried by fleas that infest rats could be controlled only through some understanding of the ecology of rats. The mosquitoes that spread malaria cannot be dealt with apart from their full natural environment.

Gradually the idea has taken hold that the health of nature carries along with it the health of mankind. Man survives only as a member of the total community. His food, safety, and well-being are linked with the welfare of all other living things.

In some branches of science, man acquires immense power to change the earth. In other scientific studies—such as ecology —he can find greater wisdom in using that power for the benefit of earth's living community.

By scientifically prolonging human life, man has rapidly increased his numbers on earth—without solving the problem of feeding them all. In applying the principles of ecology to food production, there is greater hope for the half of the earth's people who still live in hunger and want.

Modern man's advances in technology have led to the pollution of the air and water of many regions. Ecology offers some guidance in restoring healthful conditions.

In modern times, man has become the greatest challenge to his own survival. With nuclear weapons, he has become capable of turning vast areas—or even the earth itself—into an environment where nothing can live. Ecology points instead toward goals which sustain life. Every shred of truth that this science has gathered affirms that the earth can be a peaceful and orderly community, based on the interdependence which unites the human species and links mankind with all other living things.

Man has shown great skill both in adjusting to changes in his environment and in creating new conditions in which he can live. In fact, he has made himself at home in some of the most improbable places. He can survive for long periods in the deep seas, in the frigid Antarctic, in altitudes high above the earth. He is venturing into new space environments. Man is even preparing now to transport livable communities with him to the moon, or to Mars. He is solving fantastic problems in space biology and in space ecology.

But as we face the exciting prospects of this last third of the twentieth century, many of the old problems remain. The Greek word *oikos* embraced the idea of the entire world as man's home. And there is no escape from the housekeeping duties on earth. "What is the use of a house," Thoreau asked, two hundred years ago, "if you haven't got a tolerable planet to put it on?"

As we explore new worlds, we are obliged to keep this old one livable. Man is superbly fitted for the earth. It is up to him to keep it a fit place in which to live.

Suggestions for Further Reading

Bates, Marston. *The Forest and the Sea.* Random House, 1960.
An eminent biologist unfolds the drama of living things within their natural habitats, showing man's place in the pageant of nature.

Blond, Georges. *The Great Migrations* (translated by Frances Frenaye). Macmillan, 1956.
A beautifully written account of the flight of geese, the migrations of herring and salmon, of buffalo, and of locusts, and the suicidal march of the lemmings.

Cooper, Elizabeth K. *Science on the Shores and Banks.* Harcourt, 1960.
This book reveals life in a particular type of setting and offers guidance on how to observe and collect forms of plant and animal life found in, on, or near bodies of water.

Darling, Lois and Louis. *The Science of Life.* World, 1961.
A readable introduction to biology, from the single-celled organisms to man. Diagrams and drawings help explain the text.

Darwin, Charles. *The Voyage of the Beagle* (abridged by Millicent Selsam). Harper, 1959.
Darwin tells in his own words how he searched for an understanding of the origin and development of the enormous variety of living things on earth.

Dubos, René. *The Unseen World.* Rockefeller Institute Press, 1962.
A renowned microbiologist describes various types of cells and viruses, and reveals how microorganisms interact with other forms of life.

Farb, Peter, and Editors of *Life. Ecology.* Time, Inc., 1963.
An excellent study of the interrelationships of all organisms, profusely illustrated with photographs, diagrams, and drawings.

Fitzpatrick, Frederick L. *Our Animal Resources.* Holt, 1963.
The author relates the many ways in which man makes use of animals, and stresses the need for managing our biological resources wisely.

Hyde, Margaret O. *Animal Clocks and Compasses.* McGraw-Hill, 1960.
The natural rhythms by which animals live are discussed, including periodic migrations, hibernation, and changes in color.

Lavine, Sigmund A. *Strange Partners.* Little, Brown, 1960.
An account of the unusual partnerships which many animals form to secure food and shelter, aid in traveling, and safety for their young.

Matthiessen, Peter. *Wildlife in America.* The Viking Press, 1959.
A comprehensive historical survey of American wildlife, from the period of colonization to the present day, that tells of the decimation of important species.

Udall, Stewart L. *The Quiet Crisis.* Holt, 1963.
A history of the conservation movement in America, proposing a program for the wise use of our natural resources to restore a pleasant, healthy, and fruitful environment, despite the many mistakes made in the past in dealing with the bounty of nature.

Index